Also by Michael Downing

FICTION

A Narrow Time
Mother of God
Perfect Agreement
Breakfast with Scot

NONFICTION

Shoes Outside the Door

DRAMA

The Last Shaker

SPRING FORWARD

SPRING FORWARD

The Annual Madness of Daylight Saving

MICHAEL DOWNING

 Shoemaker & Hoard · Washington, D.C.

Library of Congress Cataloging-in-Publication Data
Downing, Michael.
Spring forward : the annual madness of daylight saving / Michael Downing.
p. cm.
Includes bibliographical references and index.
ISBN 1-59376-053-1 (alk. paper)
1. Daylight saving. 2. Daylight saving—United States. I. Title.
HN49.D3D69 2005
389'.17—dc22
2004025457

Book design by Mark McGarry, Texas Type & Book Works
Set in Fairfield

Printed in the United States of America

Shoemaker S&H Hoard
A Division of Avalon Publishing Group, Inc.
Distributed by Publishers Group West

10 9 8 7 6 5 4 3 2 1

For Ceil Toupin,
my timeless friend

Lose an hour in the morning, and you will spend all day looking for it.

— RICHARD WHATELY, 1854

Contents

Preface

It was a Saturday night in October. I knew I was supposed to wait until 2 A.M. on Sunday, but I was tired, and no one else
was likely to consult the kitchen clock before sunrise, so I turned
back the time by one hour. And I realized I had no idea what I was
doing.

"You were breaking the law," a neighbor told me, when I con-
fessed to him on Sunday morning. He offered to lie for me if the
Feds came around asking questions.

I wasn't seeking an alibi. I wanted to understand my crime.

During the next week, I asked a lot of people if they understood
exactly what we'd done to our clocks, or why. No one did, but a lot of
them blamed the farmers. None of us actually knew any farmers.
And if we talked about it for any length of time, most of us realized
we didn't know why farmers would want to delay the time of sunrise

from April through October, when everyone in the Northern Hemisphere enjoys later sunsets than, say, in January.

"Because they don't need more sun in January. Farmers don't farm in the snow," explained one friend. Which made sense until he added, "Of course, it doesn't snow much in Texas or Florida."

Were we saving daylight when the sunrise was earlier or when it was later? Unclear. When had Americans started to fuss with their clocks? Also unclear. Who saved what when?

One of my friends, a devoted fan of long, late summer evenings, asked me to stop talking to her about Daylight Saving. "It hurts my head when I try to think about it," she said, "and I am starting to think maybe it's a bad idea. Plus, I can't remember whether I am supposed to be tired after I change my clocks in the spring or the fall. If days are longer in summer, shouldn't we gain an hour when we Spring Forward?"

"You can change the hour of sunrise, but you can't change the time of sunrise," I said. I was quoting a very thin, serious man I'd met at a dinner party. He was a financial wizard and had a rigorous meditation practice. "Time is quantifiable, but that doesn't mean time is a quantity."

I looked at my friend to see if I was making sense. She was cradling her head in her hands.

I persisted, and a number of my friends stopped taking my calls. Others told me to lay off the farmers and pick on the other perpetrators of Daylight Saving—bus-riding schoolchildren, big-government liberals, and Richard Nixon. This seemed an unlikely coalition, but I Googled the culprits. "We still observe Daylight Savings [sic] Time largely because the FDR-mentality socialists tell us it must be a money-saving proposition or else FDR would not have created it," opined one of the thousands of columnists and bloggers I encountered who consider Daylight Saving a conspiratorial infringement on their natural rights or an insult to God. The writer had adopted the suggestive pseudonym Jon Christian Ryter. He came to typify for me the anger and confusion the topic stirred up in many Americans. And like most of his compatriots, he also added an unnecessary *s* to *Daylight Saving,* perhaps because the plural made the whole proposition seem even more preposterous. "Not only does Daylight Savings [sic] Time not 'save' anything," he wrote in October 2003, but he mysteriously alleged that "in today's communal lifestyle it actually costs every American a few bucks or more a day during the summer months."

The very thought of Daylight Saving Time seemed to give a lot of people a terrible headache, which made them mad, which made them more likely to make things up. According to Ryter, "the farmers liked it. It made sense to them.... But the utopians were absolutely convinced that the savings they gleaned in agrarian America were applicable in urban America." And though he blamed Richard Nixon for "the grandest time shuffling experiment of all time," he still considered Daylight Saving "one of those ongoing liberal myths.... In the view of the ecoalarmist, 'time shuffling' conserves the world's resources. It doesn't."

I didn't know much, but I was pretty sure Richard Nixon wasn't a true-blue liberal. And a colleague at work had mentioned that she'd always heard that farmers hated Daylight Saving Time. She had family in Iowa, which is the equivalent of a Ph.D. in agriculture, so I began to have some serious doubts about the few things I thought I knew. I decided a little more research was in order. Also, I was having trouble reaching my friends by telephone or e-mail.

A quick search of the Worldwide Web made it clear that Daylight Saving as we practice it in the United States began in World War I, World War II, in the early years of the American intervention in Vietnam, at the height of the energy crisis of the early 1970s, or during Ronald Reagan's presidency. It was first proposed by a Pittsburgh industrialist, Woodrow Wilson, a man on a horse in London, a Manhattan socialite, Benjamin Franklin, one of the Caesars, or the anonymous makers of ancient Chinese water clocks.

The confusion about Daylight Saving Time was worldwide. It even confounded the British, who like to think of themselves as the originators of the scheme. "To the clear-headed it is incredible," editorialized the London *Times* in March 1947, "that anyone should have to think whether he must put his watch an hour backwards or forwards." Although they had been observing Daylight Saving every year for thirty years by then, there were still many "muddle-headed" Brits "who have annually to decide whether they are to gain or lose an hour's sleep." A few days later, a reader alerted the editors of the *Times* to a solution: "There is a *memoria technica* for 'The Annual Problem' of shifting clock hands. It is: 'Spring forward, Fall back.' Your constant reader, Archimedes."

It was a memorable mnemonic, but by 1947, the Daylight dilemma in America was much screwier than even Archimedes could have imagined. The United States Congress had already twice passed and repealed a national Daylight Saving act, and many state legislatures annually entertained both new Daylight Saving legislation and new or stricter prohibitions against the practice. Major league baseball was pitted against the moviemakers in Hollywood. The much maligned and misunderstood farmers had even taken their case to the Supreme Court, which ruled decisively, but fueled the controversy rather than quelling it.

That one unaccountable hour consumed a lot of energy. It became a burning political, religious, and financial issue, and as any wildfire will, it took its toll. By 1965, after the debate about Daylight had roiled for more than fifty years, word came from the U.S. Naval Laboratory—the most eminent and strategically significant center for the calibration of time in the country—that the dissension over Daylight Saving had made the world's greatest economic and military superpower the world's worst timekeeper.

All this, and Richard Nixon waiting in the wings.

It seems like such a simple gesture. Spring forward, fall back. Does anyone know what we're doing?

SPRING FORWARD

Chapter One

The Infinite Hour

In a minute there is time
For decisions and revisions which a minute will reverse.

—T. S. ELIOT, 1917

Sunlight is a boon to us all, and sunlight is a limited commodity. Why waste it? This was the simple logic of Daylight Saving Time.

Although the federal government has long enjoyed a reputation for squandering the nation's resources, in 1918, the U.S. House of Representatives voted 252 to 40 to pass a law "To Save Daylight." The idea was simple. From late spring to early autumn, the sun rose before most people did, and it set before they were ready to go to sleep. Many people repelled the first light of day with shutters and shades and later relied on candles and electric lights to illuminate their evenings. Why not shift that first, unwelcome hour of light from the morning to the evening? If the nation's timepieces were simply advanced by one hour, the apparent time of both sunrise and sunset would be delayed. In effect, the nation would have one less hour of light before noon, and one more hour of light after noon. On

Thursday, 15 March 1918, this is what the Congress asked Americans to do.

It was easier done than said.

The next day, the *New York Times* capped off its yearlong editorial campaign on behalf of Daylight Saving with an attempt to quell anxiety about the controversial federal mandate. "The new daylight saving system will work out in practice as follows: The man who leaves his home at 8 o'clock in the morning will still leave at 8 by the clock, but at 7 by sun time, but when the man goes home at 5 o'clock in the afternoon by the clock he will be going home at 4 o'clock sun time, and those people who work until 6 o'clock throughout the country will be going home at 5 o'clock sun time, but it will still be 6 o'clock by the clock."

Confusion attended Daylight Saving from the start, and federal legislation didn't resolve it. Instead, the new law galvanized the opposition, an unlikely coalition of miners and farmers, Populists and Republicans, ministers and movie moguls—individuals with competing economic ambitions and contradictory political agendas. When the Congress poked its finger into the face of every clock in the country, millions of Americans winced. United by a determination to beat back the big hand of government, the opponents of Daylight Saving raised holy hell, vowing to return the nation to real time, normal time, farm time, sun time—the time they liked to think of as "God's time."

"Nobody is opposed to it," insisted the *New York Times,* three weeks before the nation's first Daylight Saving law took effect, "except possibly a few people who are opposed on principle to any alteration of established habits." Like almost everything ever uttered about Daylight Saving, this wasn't true; however, it was an honest attempt to slander the scheme's opponents as foes of progress. And there were millions of self-proclaimed conservatives on the other side. The *Springfield (Mass.) Republican* spoke for many of them when it noted that President Woodrow Wilson, a Democrat, "has indorsed the daylight saving plan. Perhaps he sympathizes with the average man, who cannot save anything else, with the present high cost of living."

Before it became the law, Daylight Saving was considered a joke. Even today, even its most ardent advocates believe that when Ben Franklin took pen in hand and wrote the first detailed proposal to save daylight—a 1784 letter to the editors of the *Journal of Paris*—he had his tongue in his cheek. Franklin called for a tax on every Parisian window shuttered after sunrise to "encourage the economy of using sunshine instead of candles." Replete with calculations of the hypothetical savings in wax and tallow, Franklin's modest proposal is furnished with a crude method of enforcement. "Every morning, let all the bells in every church be set ringing; and if that is not sufficient?, let cannon be fired in every street, to wake the sluggards effectually, and make them open their eyes to see their true interest."

But thrift was never a joke to Franklin. The idea of saving daylight had first occurred to him in London thirty years earlier, as he recalls in *The Autobiography*. "I observ'd there was not one shop open tho' it had been Day-light & the Sun up above three Hours. The Inhabitants of London chusing voluntarily to live much by Candle Light, and sleep by Sunshine; and yet often complain a little absurdly, of the Duty on Candles and the high Price of Tallow." Conceding that individual citizens might consider the cost of candles and lamp oil "trifling Matters not worth minding," Franklin urged these wastrels to remember that, as with any small saving, "the great Number of Instances in a populous City, and its frequent Repetition give it Weight & Consequence; perhaps they will not censure very severely those who bestow some Attention to Affairs of this seemingly low nature."

As usual, Franklin's call for moderation was ignored. It was not until 1909 that the first American Daylight Saving legislation was drafted. And its sponsors were severely censured. When they brought their proposal to the floor of the House of Representatives, "they were repulsed," noted a congressional observer for the London *Times*. "The statement may be hazarded that the House will reject the proposal as 'freak legislation.'" By then, Daylight Saving had already established itself as a perennial legislative loser in Britain.

The uncanny idea of falsifying clocks to delay the apparent time of sunset had been hatched by the English architect William Willett. An avid golfer and hunter, Willett rode his horse through the deserted streets of London every day at dawn. Most Londoners were asleep, he noticed, and their windows were shuttered. One morning, the first rays of sunshine struck him like a bolt of lightning—according to the legend perpetrated by Willett and his admirers, which resembles in its details the conversion of Saul of Tarsus, who was temporarily blinded by a heavenly light on his way to persecute some Christians and turned into St. Paul, propagator of the faith. And Willett sounded like a man on an apostolic crusade. "Light is one of the great gifts of the Creator," he wrote. "Against our ever-besieging enemy, disease, light and fresh air act as guards in our defence, and when the conflict is close, supply us with the most effective weapons with which to overcome the invader."

Willett's epiphany—"the sun shines upon the land for several hours each day while we are asleep, and is rapidly nearing the horizon, having already passed its western limit, when we reach home after the work day is over"—turned him into a missionary. In 1907, he published his influential pamphlet, "The Waste of Daylight," which included a detailed proposal for "The Daylight Saving Act," and was appended by dozens of endorsements from prominent British esquires and honorables. Willett wanted to push the clocks ahead by eighty minutes every spring to increase people's exposure to the healing properties of sunlight. He brought to this proposal a convert's enthusiasm and a marked inability to distinguish between the sublime and the ridiculous. "That so many as 210 hours of daylight are to all intents and purposes wasted every year, is a defect in our civilisation. Let England recognise and remedy it," he wrote, promising that the "benefits afforded by parks and open spaces will be doubled," and "opportunities for rifle practice will have been created, which under existing conditions cannot be contemplated."

When the editors of the *New York Times* first heard about this proposal in 1907, they pronounced Willett's idea "little less than an act of madness." Soldiering on against his critics, Willett did seem more than a little Quixotic. "Even the blind keenly realize the difference between the daylight and darkness," he claimed. "They are always cheered by the former, but depressed by the latter." British legislators first debated and roundly rejected the Daylight Saving Act in 1908. Willett got right back on his horse, lobbying and lecturing for the cause until his death in 1915. He did not live to see the day when "everyone, rich and poor alike will find their ordinary expenditure on electric light, gas, oil, and candles considerably reduced." When the House of Parliament entertained a 1916 version of Willett's proposal, which would have required citizens to alter their clocks four times—skipping ahead twenty minutes every Sunday in April to achieve "Summer Time" incrementally—Britain's Royal Astronomer was still joking about it. He expressed his disapproval by tacking on an amendment to make winters warmer: "And let it be further enacted," he wrote, "that between the months of October and March the thermometer should be put up ten degrees."

But the outbreak of World War I in 1914 had tempered the British sense of humor, and the Royal Astronomer's clause was ruled out of order. Parliament passed a revised draft of the 1916 Daylight Act, which was to take effect April 1917. No one gave a nod to Ben Franklin's comic inspiration—that the sun *gave light as soon as he rose. This is what I claim as my discovery."* Franklin had expected "neither place, pension, exclusive privilege, nor any other reward whatever" for his part in saving daylight. "I expect only to have the

honour of it." William Willett expected even less. He had also
eschewed fame and personal profit, but he lacked Franklin's light
touch, piously predicting that the first nation to enact his proposal
would enjoy "the honour of bringing similar blessings within easier
reach of a great proportion of mankind." Willett believed, in his
small way, that he had contributed to the greatness of Great Britain.

Britain's finest hour was spoiled by a German sneak attack. "'German Summer Time' began on Monday," reported the London *Times*
in early May 1916. Trying to assuage this injury to English pride, the
Times noted that, in Germany, "the change required no legislation,
but was merely 'ordained' by the Federal Council in the exercise of
powers which it enjoys during the war." The Germans shrugged off
the criticism of their undemocratic process and gleefully reported
that "the change has been well received, and is regarded as an
appropriate stimulus to war work." Frankfurt's daily *Zeitung*
acknowledged the decade-long British debate about Daylight Saving,
but added, "it is characteristic of England that she could not rouse
herself to a decision."

"While daylight surrounds us," wrote William Willett, "cheerfulness
reigns." His vision of the peaceable kingdom did not come to pass.
But by the time the United States declared war on Germany in the
spring of 1917, more than a dozen European nations had adopted
some form of his Daylight Saving plan. The scheme's American
advocates, who had long been dismissed as caddies for the interests
of the leisure class, shifted the battle from the golf links to the
trenches. "Millions of dollars will be saved by the people of the
United States," announced the newly elected president of the American Association for the Advancement of Science, "and our 'preparedness' along industrial lines will be augmented." He predicted
an annual saving of $25 million in energy costs. He achieved this figure by unscientifically doubling a dubious British estimate of $12.5

million in fuel conservation during Great Britain's first year of Daylight Saving. Plus, as he pointed out, $25 million was "enough to build two super-dreadnoughts each year."

Even under normal circumstances, it would have been difficult to calculate the fuel economy achieved by Daylight Saving. Energy consumption is notoriously variable from year to year, fluctuating as unpredictably as the weather. During World War I, credit for the total fuel saving should have been impossible to sort out, as consumption was severely restricted by the industrial conservation programs and civilian rationing measures the federal government had imposed. Within a year, though, Daylight advocates upped the ante, claiming that the scheme would save the United States $1 per citizen per year, or $110 million. And contrary to the established principles of economics, it was touted by the *New York Times* as "the only reform ever proposed that did not involve expenditures by somebody . . . the only one that didn't involve the making of money by somebody."

The rhetoric of the campaign to impose Daylight Saving on the United States was distinguished by deliberate misrepresentation and preposterous exaggeration. "Among the *Fifty-Two Convincing Reasons for the Daylight Saving Bill,"* according to the May 1918 issue of *Current Opinion,* were "expediting the training of the national forces, speeding up production in the plants making war material and stimulating work in the ship-building yards." Precisely how the primitive gesture of mechanically altering clock time would increase the pace and efficiency of all human endeavors went undocumented. But it seemed to become true by repetition. "General efficiency will, of course, be increased by any improvement in the health, morals and social welfare of the workers," asserted the report of the Special Committee on Daylight Saving Plan, prepared for Congress by the Boston Chamber of Commerce. The logic of the campaign was circular, which made it easier to spin. "That children will profit by the change hardly needs to be urged," asserted these Bostonians, who also foresaw great advantages for the most vulnerable members of the society. "Working mothers and fathers obtain an extra hour for outdoor play with their children.... Working girls will be on the way home in the daylight instead of the dark," and there would be "lessened eye-strain for workers and school children ... lessened risk of accident in industrial establishments ... lessened risk of accident due to transportation and traffic conditions."

On the other side, the rhetoric of the campaign to defeat Daylight Saving was distinguished by deliberate misrepresentation and preposterous exaggeration. The opponents foresaw the disruption of international trade and the discombobulation of transcontinental communications. Moreover, "it upsets all astronomical data, making the almanac almost useless. It causes great confusion in the navy and the merchant marine service." These arguments from isolationists might have been more persuasive if Americans did not share their seas and skies and telegraph lines with Canadians and Europeans, who were already observing Daylight Saving. But by 1918, the popular objections to Daylight Saving had congealed into a kind of litany of illogic, which was repeated in thousands of letters written to newspapers that spring, as Congress debated the fate of the national legislation. "It prevents people from enjoying the air in the morning, when it is fresh and healthful, by compelling them to go in shop or office one hour before it is necessary," warned one naysayer from Brooklyn. "It upsets the schedule of all large manufacturing plants, as their working hours are arranged so as to take advantage of the summer daylight hours. It is the direct cause of overcrowding of transit lines during rush hours, as it causes everybody to go to work at the same time, where as under normal conditions different factories have different arrangement of working hours, thereby lessening the overcrowding of cars."

The mechanics of Daylight Saving were devastatingly simple, but both sides were confounded by the physics of the proposition. How could you save time by losing an hour? If you were "springing forward," why did you end up delaying the time of sunrise and sunset?

And why not save daylight in the winter, when there is a lot less of it? From the cacophony of questions and confusion across the country, there emerged a kind of chaotic public debate, with both sides attempting to commodify the time that would be lost or gained. The president of the American Association for the Advancement of Science premised his enthusiastic endorsement on the inarguable benefits of more light—"light is a physical stimulus," he said, "just as darkness is a depressive influence"—as if Daylight Saving could actually increase the amount of available light on the planet. Testifying before the Welfare Committee of the New York Board of Aldermen, a Mrs. Dunlap attempted a more humble defense of the home front. "She opposed it because it made the housewife prepare supper in the hottest part of the day and the laborer had to go to bed in the hottest part of the evening," effectively losing an hour of much needed sleep. Not so, replied the advocates. "Our last hour of sleep will be sounder and more beneficial than it is under present conditions because there will be less light." Not so, replied the dissenters. "It robs everyone of two hours' sleep, as one hour in the morning, when it is cool and restful, is worth two hours in the evening, when it is hot and restless, thereby causing a great increase in the nervous diseases."

One thing was certain: From the beginning, it was absolutely unnecessary. Everybody knew it. "Daylight saving was brought about by a shift of the clock applying to the whole country," observed a university professor in the *American Economic Review*, "although theoretically all that was necessary was for each individual to get up an hour earlier and make his day's progress on that basis!" In the *International Journal of Ethics*, a legal scholar dubbed the peculiar annual ritual of altering clock time a "modern expedient," an exercise in efficiency. "Rather than change all the hours of work, the community prefers to employ a simple fiction as to the time," he hypothesized. But you didn't need an advanced degree to see what was really hap-

pening. A letter writer to the *New York Times* compared Daylight
Saving to "a man cheating himself at solitaire and thinking he has
won." And when his hometown of Portage, Wisconsin, decided to
"spring forward" and join the rest of the nation on "fast time,"
Charles Gale simply refused to adjust his timepieces, reported the
New York World. "I'm fooled enough," he told his daughter, "without
fooling myself on purpose."

Before Daylight Saving became law, the combatants in the preposterous public debate had torn apart the twinned ideals of God and
Country and divvied them up. "Changing the clock," argued the
opponents, "was flying in the face of Providence." In another historical moment, that might have been a winning argument. But bullets
and bombs were flying across Europe, and Congress had declared
war on Germany, so Daylight's proponents wrapped themselves in
the flag, appropriated the war effort, and successfully turned the
House vote in March 1918 into a loyalty test. And they won.

Soon, though, above the din of the nationalistic jingo, Americans
heard the jangle of coins in the pockets of those patriots. The lofty
humanitarian goals of Daylight Saving—to get working girls safely
home before dark, to reunite dads and moms with the kids before
shadows fell on the backyard garden, to safeguard the physical and
mental health of industrial workers by increasing their daily opportunity for sports and recreation—also resembled an innovative strategy
for boosting retail sales. It was not exactly for nothing that chambers
of commerce and other merchants' associations had figured among
the earliest and staunchest supporters of Daylight Saving. The most
powerful members of these civic organizations, the giant department
stores—arguably the most significant economic institutions on the
urban landscape—were also the most significant source of advertising revenue for urban newspapers, whose editors were eventually
converted to the Daylight cause.

In the spring of 1918, the opportunists knocked, besieging Americans with new ways to squander their anticipated savings. "A reliable clock with a loud alarm is the best way of making sure you will not be an hour behind time, when the plan goes into effect," advised one of the thousands of newspaper advertisements placed by department stores eager to capitalize on the confusion. "Alarm clocks at Bamberger's, some with radium dials, priced from 1.15 to 4.50." Working girls were encouraged to stop and shop on their way home to update their wardrobes with dresses specifically designed for the brighter summer evenings. "The French call it the five-to-midnight ensemble," announced the *New York Times* in an article about the new neither-day-nor-nighttime fashions. "We in America are more prone to speak of it as a daylight-dining ensemble." Daylight specials offered discounts on garden spades, watering cans, baseball bats, golf clubs, and even new homes. "Daylight Saving means an extra rest hour each afternoon to every business man," proclaimed one Long Island residential-development ad that ran daily in New York newspapers throughout the spring. "Will you waste this chance for wholesome country by living in the stuffy city?"

If you didn't want to purchase any patriotic paraphernalia, there was somebody prepared to sell you some leisure. The secretary of baseball's National League foresaw "sixty minutes of extra sunshine a day for the people of the United States during the five best months in the year for outdoor sports and recreation. It will be a means of drawing more people to the game, and the national pastime should thrive accordingly. There will be fewer games called on account of darkness and the more or less discomfort of trying to follow the contest in the twilight of the Fall will be obviated." By early 1918, several professional baseball teams had begun to revise their schedules to take advantage of the extended evenings and boost attendance. This maneuver incited the ire of the estimable Charles Lathrop Pack, who called both the National and American leagues to task. In a forcefully worded rebuke, he reminded them that the "law was intended to increase the daylight usefulness in war work, and was not intended to give extra hours for recreation. . . . Slackers of the worst type is the brand placed upon baseball league owners or managers who plan to move down the schedule time of starting games this Summer." Charles Lathrop Pack was something of a player himself. As historian Michael O'Malley points out in *Keeping Watch,* in 1918, Pack was president of the War Garden Commission, a patriotically named "lobbying organization for the makers of garden products—tools, seeds, fertilizers, canning and preserving equipment . . . who stood to gain dramatically from any increase in wartime gardening."

It should have been a fad—the hula hoop of government programs. That's how these stories typically turn out: One man's lonely passion meets with ridicule and then catches on, and finally the novelty is pumped up with possibilities and expectations and ambitions until it is so wildly overinflated it simply explodes. Bloated as it was with hot air from both sides, Daylight Saving proved to be resilient; it just grew and grew and grew into an ever bigger problem.

There was no shortage of contemporary controversies competing for people's affections and disaffections. Women didn't have the vote, children were working without the benefit of labor laws, Bolsheviks seemed to be sneaking into every city, the Black Sox scandal had tainted baseball, and you couldn't get a decent drink anywhere in the country. By passing the Volstead Act and ratifying the Eighteenth Amendment to the Constitution, the same Congress that passed the Daylight law and led a reluctant nation to war also forbade the sale, import, or export of intoxicating liquors.

But the war did end. And in 1920, the Nineteenth Amendment resolved the century-long struggle for equal suffrage by granting women the vote. In 1921, major league baseball appointed a commissioner to keep itself clean. By 1933, even Prohibition was put to rest with the passage of the Twenty-First Amendment. But in 1937, when anthropologist Margaret Mead was in Bali studying the indigenous people's public-opinion mechanisms, she deemed them to be quite logical when compared with "our society's tradition of emotional involvement in every type of issue, from the revision of the Constitution to Daylight Saving Time."

Nothing fuels a controversy like confusion, and another thirty years later, after another world war had been fought, passions on both sides of the Daylight debate were still enflamed and the nation was absurdly out of sync with itself. In 1965, eighteen states observed Daylight Saving, so that their clocks ran one hour ahead of Standard Time for six months of the year; eighteen other states half-heartedly participated, which meant that the clocks in some cities and towns in these states ran one hour ahead of Standard Time for periods ranging from three to six months every year and some didn't; twelve states did not practice Daylight Saving at all, keeping their clocks one hour behind the clocks in the observant states; and in areas of Texas and North Dakota, local residents adopted "daylight in reverse," so that their clocks ran one hour behind Standard Time, and two hours behind Daylight Saving Time. In that year, *The Nation* estimated that "100 million Americans were out of step with the other 80 million" and quoted a U.S. Naval Observatory official who had dubbed the United States "the world's worst timekeeper."

The controversy was not limited to exotic locations or the esoteric domains of science and technology. It was still heating up the heartland of America. In 1966, while campaigning on behalf of a Republican candidate for the House of Representatives in Council Bluffs, Iowa, the scandal magnet Richard Nixon immediately attracted the attention of unhappy farmers. The *New York Times* reported that "one of the big issues out here is daylight saving time," which the Democratic governor had recently reimposed on Iowans for the first time in almost fifty years. "Mr. Nixon, speaking at a breakfast rally, began by saying it seemed terribly early. It was 11 A.M. central daylight time or 10 A.M. standard time, referred to here as

God's time. 'But what time is it?' Mr. Nixon asked. 'I'm confused.'
This brought laughter from the audience." How confusing it must
have been for those Iowa farmers seven years later, when Nixon
embraced Daylight Saving more wholeheartedly than had any other
president in American history.

To this day, Daylight Saving accrues dubious credit for fossil-fuel
savings and dubious blame for school bus accidents; it is seasonally
cited as a contributing factor in the ups and downs of the Dow Jones
and the Nielsen ratings. One fact is indisputable: Daylight Saving
did not displace God as the nation's timekeeper. Americans had
been forced off sun time—God's time—several decades before the
federal government attempted to create a coherent national timekeeping policy in 1918.

Standard Time was introduced to the United States by the railroads in 1883, effectively abolishing the habit of looking to the heavens for temporal guidance. And by 1918, most Americans had grown
accustomed to the inaccurate but useful shorthand of organizing
time into standardized geographic zones.

Prior to 1883, local timekeeping was more art than science. As
measured by sundials or, less precisely, by anyone looking up and
gauging the distance between the sun's position and its typical high
point at midday, sun time varies by location. Thus, before the railroads imposed Standard Time zones across the country, when it was
(apparently) noon in Chicago, it was 11:39 A.M. in St. Paul and 12:31
P.M. in Pittsburgh; when it was noon in Washington, D.C., it was
11:43 A.M. in Savannah and 12:24 P.M. in Boston. Moreover, affordable wind-up clocks and watches were not precision instruments,
and their keepers were not infallible. People typically wound and
reset their watches at least once a day, a daily occasion for losing or
gaining a few minutes. And unless they kept sundials—a technology

especially ill-suited to life in apartments stacked up along the shadowy streets of high-rising cities—people had to choose a local clock to use as their standard. Even in relatively rural areas, this was not as simple as it sounds. Was it noon when the first or the twelfth church bell bonged? Big balls—the precursors to the Times Square New Year inaugurator—were installed on towers and attached to steeples, but most people couldn't leave their homes or factories to witness the official onset of afternoon. And it mattered exactly where you were when you heard the bell or spotted the ball; in the mid–nineteenth century, the *Chicago Tribune* countenanced twenty-seven distinct local times in the state of Illinois alone.

Railroad operators attempted to iron out this mess. They instituted Railroad Time, which made it much easier for the operators of individual rail lines to produce reliable timetables. Railroad Time did not do much to ease timekeeping. Soon, America's major rail stations were festooned with clocks—one to display local time, and one clock for each rail company—each one showing a different time. In Pittsburgh, for example, six to eight different time standards governed departure and arrival times. Did the trains run on time? According to the Friendship Association of European Model Railroaders, it would have been hard to prove they didn't.

The Pennsylvania Railroad in the East used Philadelphia time, which was 5 minutes slower than New York time and 5 minutes faster than Baltimore time. The Baltimore & Ohio used Baltimore time for trains running out of Baltimore, Columbus time for trains in Ohio, Vincennes time for trains running west of Cincinnati, and it scheduled some of its trains under New York time, Philadelphia time, and Chicago time. The Michigan Central Railroad operated its trains on Detroit time. In the Chicago district the New York Central and the Pennsylvania used Columbus time which was 6 minutes faster than Cincinnati time and 19 minutes faster than Chicago time.

This was imperfect; the nation's railroads were juggling more than one hundred standard times. Several trains could depart a single station at the same moment at altogether different times. In 1883, Standard Time made it noon in Chicago and St. Paul at the same moment that it was 1 P.M. in Pittsburgh, Boston, Washington, D.C., and Savannah, creating the impression of uniform regional time-distances from east to west across the map of America. By the spring of 1918, although there were still people who refused to abandon their reckoning of sun time and did not adjust their watches or town clocks to conform to their designated time-zone time, the principle of Standard Time was well established and generally observed.

Standard Time did not become law until the federal government enacted the national legislation "To Save Daylight and to Provide Standard Time for the United States" in 1918. The congressional decision to link the formalization of Standard Time to the adoption of Daylight Saving permanently complicated the controversy that the legislation was supposed to resolve. And it didn't serve the Congress. Americans were left with the distinct impression that the bully who had torn up the biblical timetables was big government, not big business.

In categorical terms, time zones and Daylight Saving were both national initiatives designed to coordinate timekeeping practices. But whereas Standard Time had evolved over thirty-five years, Daylight Saving was a newer, more controversial, and much more mind-bending idea. And the nation was not eased into the transition. On Friday, 16 March 1918, the day after the House of Representatives passed it, the Senate approved the Daylight Saving legislation, which was an amended version of a bill the Senate had already passed. On Monday, 19 March, President Woodrow Wilson signed it into law. Less than two weeks later, citizens would be required to misalign the hands of their watches and clocks. At 2 A.M. Standard

Time on 31 March, under the cover of darkness, Americans were to make it appear that it was 3 A.M. On the last Sunday of October, again at 2 A.M., they would undo the illusion.

This single act of Congress required people to adopt Standard Time and, at the same moment, to perform a manual adjustment so that their clocks would not run on Standard Time. With Daylight Saving Time in effect, every clock in the newly legislated Standard Time zones was off by an hour, and those clocks would be wrong for seven of the twelve months of the year.

"The railroads are relieved of possible complication in the time tables by the fact that the change goes into effect at 2 A.M., which is an hour when no train leaves any of the stations in New York," reported the still optimistic *New York Times* on the day before the law took effect.

The latest train out of the Grand Central Station before 2 A.M. is one for Albany, leaving at 12:25 for Albany and scheduled, according to the time table, to arrive at 5:05. When the train gets into Albany, however it will be 6:05. The earliest train leaving the Grand Central after the change goes into effect will be a New Haven train leaving at 6 A.M.—and travelers taking this train will miss it by an hour if they fail to shove their clocks ahead in time. The Pennsylvania Railroad has a train coming in from Boston at 2:20 A.M. and leaving for Boston at 2:30 A.M. This train tomorrow morning, however, will be an hour late in arriving and an hour late in leaving, although in actual time it will not be a minute later either coming or going. On the following morning, however, the time schedules, remaining unchanged, the train arrivals and departures will fall automatically in conformance with the clocks.

According to the headline, "No Confusion Expected."

Also unexpected was the nation's decision to abandon Daylight Saving the next year.

Chapter Two

The Farmer in the Dew

It is always sunrise somewhere; the dew is never all dried at once.
—JOHN MUIR, 1938

In 1995, more than seventy-five years after the original Daylight Saving legislation was passed and repealed, a woman in Bellevue, Washington, was anticipating "that fateful day, Oct. 29, when all clocks 'fall behind.'" Like many Americans crowded into cities along the nation's west and east coasts, she understood that "Daylight Savings Time [sic] was instituted for the benefit of farmers who needed more daylight for chores." It was, she told the editors of the *New York Times,* an anachronism. "Now, agribusiness has arranged matters so that daylight hours don't matter; cows are milked by machine. . . . It's time to decide on one or the other time permanently. Yes, other countries, like Britain, change hours. But they still have small farms, where more daylight matters." She concluded her diatribe against the farmers and their outdated time scheme with a nod to modern science. "We need more daylight in winter, not summer, as chronobiologists will tell you."

Every year, in April and October, these tirades rise like a tide. Angry letters pour into newspapers from New York to San Francisco ("because of a stupid law from the 19th century with the welfare of farmers in mind who need to get up at an ungodly hour to tend animals, we are inflicted with the loss of a precious hour of daylight!"), weblogs around the world roil with complaints ("Why do we have to do this? Because it gives the farmers more light in the morning. . . . Why can't the fuckwit farmers just set their bloody alarms back an hour and get out of bed earlier? Why must the whole population suffer for their stupidity and laziness?"), and advice columns are flooded with variations on the simple questions posed by a young reader to the Argonne National Laboratory's *Ask a Scientist* Web site:

> Doug: What is the purpose of Daylight Saving Time? . . . Why can't we just leave time alone?
>
> Professor Topper: The purpose is to maximize daylight hours for farmers so that they can get their work done and still overlap nicely with the rest of the world . . . at least, this is what I was always told.

In 1917, American farmers were told the same story. They weren't listening. From the first, farmers opposed Daylight Saving, which was an urban idea of a good idea, hatched in London and cultivated in the cities of Europe and the northern United States. England's farmers had objected strenuously to "messing the clock about." When the British began saving daylight in 1917, farmers across England adopted resolutions for its repeal. In Northampton, at "the largest meeting of farmers held in the town in many years," their plight under the new time was explained by a dairyman to a *Times* correspondent. "His men had to begin work at half-past four in order to get the milk from 17 cows to Weedon Barracks by a quarter to 7. The barracks authority had told him that they would now require the milk at 6 o'clock, and he had asked them to fetch it, as he did not intend to alter his arrangements."

By 1919, the residents of New York and other American cities fetched their milk in bottles from the front porch or the corner store. Provisions were the provenance of shopkeepers, bankers, doctors, lawyers, and other merchants, the typical members of the local chamber of commerce. And they wanted Daylight Saving. These businessmen were not assembly-line workers or unionized laborers— "They play golf," said Congressman Edward King of Illinois—but they were organized. By 1912, independent merchants' associations and commercial clubs from Pittsburgh to Seattle had organized themselves under a central administration, the United States Chamber of Commerce. "I do not desire to say anything against the chambers of commerce," declared Congressman King, "but it is a known fact that they have got one of the best lobbying institutions for legislation in Congress—I do not say corruptly—that has ever been conceived."

The chamber of commerce campaign on behalf of Daylight Saving was supported by a widely circulated analysis compiled in 1917 by the Boston Chamber of Commerce, whose chairman, A. Lincoln Filene, owned Boston's biggest department store. The thirty-page pamphlet, "An Hour of Light for an Hour of Night," identified sixteen benefits to health, morals, social welfare, efficiency, and the economy, most of which accrued to city dwellers—potential retail customers. However, Filene's report also laid out ten distinct advantages that would be enjoyed specifically by farmers and their families, a list "approved by the Massachusetts Board of Agriculture and several prominent farmers." Two of these ten blessings were a matter of dew:

—Fruit and vegetables and many agricultural products handled early in the morning are far superior to those which the sun has been shining on for some time.

—Most farm products are better when gathered with dew on. They are firmer, crisper, than if the sun has dried the dew off.

The beneficence of morning dew was news to most farmers. They did see appreciably more dew after the clocks had been shoved ahead. This stood to reason. In April 1917, the farmer who went to milk his cows at 5:00 A.M. could see the sun beginning to spread over his fields and dry them out. In April 1918, the same farmer rising and milking at the same time had to wait an extra hour for the sun to appear and dry the dew. And unlike Mr. Filene, the farmer liked his dew dried. "There are many crops that cannot be harvested or handled until the dew has dried off," complained a Connecticut farmer, who told the *New York Times* he found himself wasting "practically half the forenoon" with Daylight Saving. A farmer in Cedar Gap, Missouri, dubbed it "The Daylight Robbing Law" because "the cutting of grass and cereals, as well as the picking of fruit is almost impossible till the sun is pretty well up."

With the exception of the "prominent farmers" consulted by the Boston Chamber of Commerce, this dim view of dew was shared by agricultural workers in Massachusetts. Within a few years, in fact, the farmers of the Massachusetts State Grange appealed to the Supreme Court for relief, contending that the state's Daylight Saving law had cost farmers $20 million and "was unconstitutional because it deprived persons of property without compensation and was otherwise obnoxious."

The dew debate did not evaporate, even as World War I staggered toward its uneasy conclusion. A general armistice was declared in Europe on 11 November 1918; the Daylight Saving law remained in effect, and Americans sprang ahead for the second time. "The equinoctial ceremony of putting forward the clock has passed off, in the case of this country without friction," observed *The Nation* in April 1919, "save for a growl from the farmer who anticipates trouble with his hired hand and his cow." Congress was not deaf to discontent among dairymen; a lot of elected officials liked their bread buttered. And by the time President Woodrow Wilson went to France to sign the Treaty of Versailles in June 1919 and officially end the war, Congress had turned its attention from the battlefield to the barnyard.

The most significant legislative effort to repeal Daylight Saving was framed as a rider and attached to the annual agricultural appropriations bill. In May and June 1919, the House of Representatives convened a series of hearings on Daylight Saving. Farmers dominated the debate, vowing to repeal the law, and permanently wedding themselves to Daylight Saving in the public's imagination. The fact that the public forgot which side the farmers were on is absolutely not the public's fault. By the end of the 1919 hearings, most congressmen had forgotten which side they themselves had been on the previous year.

The devastating disadvantages reported to Congress by farmers suffering under Daylight Saving Time corresponded precisely to the advantages predicted by the Boston Chamber of Commerce. According to that analysis, "farmers who go to market would come into better relations, as far as daylight is concerned, with city buyers, as it is customary for farmers to arrive at market early in the morning, and the city day does not generally conform in any respects to that of the farmer." Apparently, the Bostonians had not consulted many cows.

Cows liked to be milked at twelve-hour intervals, and farmers were long accustomed to waking before sunrise in the winter months to procure the milk they sold to nearby cities and towns. Daylight Saving forced these farmers up before sunrise in the summer, as well, which precipitated other problems. These problems were universally recognized. As an English dairyman had explained to the *Times* of London, "the drawback is that much of the early morning work at the homestead . . . will have to be done by artificial light, which means additional expense." In Illinois, as Congressman King explained to his colleagues in the House of Representatives, the farmer had to "get up at 3:30 o'clock in the morning, wake up his wife and children by stirring around the house, and has got to go out and raise the animals and 'cuss' because Congress forgot to specify any arrangement where by the cows would give down their milk any earlier, and he does not get down the full quota of milk, but what he has must go to the city on the early train." In hundreds of letters and editorials that appeared that spring and summer in urban newspapers, farmers were advised to ignore the new clock time if it caused such hardship, though even the *New York Times* eventually admitted, "They cannot ignore Daylight Saving Time if the local creamery, milk trains, mails, banks, and schools all make the change."

The Chamber of Commerce had also predicted that the advantage of turning ahead the clocks "would hold true as regards purchasing by farmers in the city." But Daylight Saving extended evening light, which naturally kept the farmer at work later than had been normal. "I have seven or eight petitions from small-town merchants asking for the repeal of this law. In order to accommodate the farmers who insist upon working, they must keep their places of business open until 10 or 11 o'clock at night and open at 7 o'clock in the morning," Representative King informed his colleagues. "The farmer cannot attend the country schoolhouse debate in the evening because he can not get there before half-past nine to save his soul."

The last of the ten advantages foreseen by the Boston Chamber of Commerce involved our four-legged friends: "In the summer and during hot weather, it is far better for animals—particularly horses—to do their work during the cool part of the day, and this could be accomplished by beginning earlier in the morning." Congressman King was not a man to be out-horse-sensed by a bunch of gentleman farmers. For starters, the cool, early part of the day is precisely what had been abbreviated by Daylight Saving. Thus, explained King, having roused himself and his whole family at 3:30, "an ungodly hour" to milk the cows, the farmer

enters the field after the dew is off at 9 or 10 o'clock and in but a little while when he looks up and hears the horn sound at the house
for dinner, the sun says it is 11 o'clock, and he must go to dinner at
11 o'clock and must bring in all the farm horses and all the help.
And then what happens? One of the most injurious things to farm
life, and that is this, that at 12 o'clock when the sun is in the meridian he must take his animals out into the fields and work them. It is
almost cruelty to animals and even to farm men to work at that hour
in the day. Yet under this law, in order to get his work done, the
farmer must do it. I know personally of a number of cases where
horses have fallen under the heat. We should have some regard for
our friend, the horse.

America's human farm population reached its historical peak of
32 million between 1910 and 1920. Traditionally, when something
rubbed farmers the wrong way, Congress generously applied salves
in the form of subsidies, artificially inflated crop prices, and a series
of land-reclamation and homesteading acts. Why, then, in 1919 were
twenty-eight bills to repeal Daylight Saving languishing in Congress?
Because the cities were better at growing populations—voters—
than were the farms.

At the end of the eighteenth century, 90 percent of Americans
had been farmers; by the end of the nineteenth century, farmers represented 43 percent of the labor force; in 1920, only one-third of the
nation's total population of 105 million was living on farms, and
farmers made up just 27 percent of the labor force. Despite a vigor-
ous back-to-the-farm movement, young men—many first drawn off
the farm by the war—were moving to cities and the promise of
eight-hour working days. The American economy needed more and
more workers who did not grow their own food; this encouraged
large-scale, automated agriculture, not more family farms.

To preserve their political clout, farmers had to be recast as a spe-

cial interest, a vital minority. "Upon our American fields and mead-
ows we have reared a great industrial structure, a veritable Tower of
Babel lifting its builders high above an immediate struggle with the
natural environment in the effort to maintain life," sermonized Ralph
Gabriel in the *North American Review,* speaking for farmers if not
exactly speaking like a farmer. Yet, he went on, "the food quest is as
vital today as it was to the primitive savage who hunted beasts in the
forest. The recent war has made this dependence very vivid. The
speed with which Babel can be built now depends on whether the
farmer increases his yields of corn and wheat."

Such grandiloquence did not serve the immediate cause of con-
trolling the clocks. It reinforced the popular impression of farmers as
old-fashioned fundamentalists. More worrisome, this rhetoric
defined Daylight Saving as a feud between city folk and their country cousins. And in a political battle that simply pitted farmers
against factory workers, the likely winner would not be holding a
hoe. Among the staunch supporters of Daylight Saving was Samuel
Gompers, president of the American Federation of Labor, "meaning
the toilers in factories, mills, and shops, big and little all over the
country," the *New York Times* reminded Congress. And with labor "is
the whole professional class and all employers not farmers. That is a
situation, which the lawmakers from the standpoint of self-interest,
and while engaged in their favorite occupation of 'balancing votes'
against each other, cannot afford to ignore."

James Strong, a freshman congressman from Kansas, heeded this
warning. When he appeared before the House hearings on the
repeal of Daylight Saving in early June 1919, he was holding two big
bundles of letters from farmers. He claimed to have ten times as
many: "I would be glad to get a dray and bring over the rest." Strong
had surveyed his constituents about their most pertinent concerns,
and "beyond their interest in the league of nations, beyond every-

thing else, except bringing the boys home from France, they wanted the daylight-saving law repealed." Instead of dividing these hard-working farmers from their more numerous brothers in the factories, however, Congressman Strong proposed an alliance. He acknowledged that Daylight Saving had been endorsed by the American Federation of Labor and other union leaders:

> They say they represent the laboring men who want this law. I think they represent the men who organized the laboring men. There is no doubt in my mind about that. The office men, Mr. Gompers and all of the others who live off the laboring men, favor the continuance of this law. But in my little town of Blue Rapids, I have 250 men who work in the gypsum mills.... They do not want to quit at 5 o'clock and play golf; they do not want to quit at 5 o'clock and indulge in amusements; they want to go home and rest, and they do not want their women to have to commence the afternoon dinner at 4 o'clock.

In the congressional lexicon, workers—on the farm or in the factory—were workers, and everyone else was a duffer. "The man who wants to go out and play tennis, golf, and ball and go fishing has an argument," said Congressman King of Illinois, "and that is the only argument I think there is in favor of keeping this obnoxious law on the statute book; to let the pleasure-seekers, the swivel-chair ornaments, and the golf players get out an hour earlier and go and play." No one who did an honest day's work in King's district could tolerate Daylight Saving. He'd heard tell of a "mass meeting" in Mendon, Illinois. "Nearly everybody attended, and they passed a resolution abolishing the daylight law as far as they were concerned." In his meeting-mad district, five hundred coal miners "met and resolved to ask for the repeal of this law, which gets them up so early in the morning, at daylight, and causes them to eat their heavy meal so early in the afternoon that they have to go to bed at night hungry."

For a few brief days in early June 1919, the workers of the world were united—at least, in the minds of those men in Washington, D.C., who represented congressional districts occupied by both farmers and industrial workers. Representative Edward Denison, a member of the House hearings committee, interrupted the testimony of a delegate from the American Federation of Labor to ask about the attitude of the United Mine Workers. "I am asking," said Denison, "because I happen to represent one of the largest coal mining districts in the United States, the southern Illinois district, and I think I have heard from and had resolutions from almost every miner's local in my district and from other districts urging me to repeal this law."

Saving coal had been the principal justification for the wartime adoption of Daylight Saving. Even if coal miners favored the repeal—which was alleged, not proved—the miners' opinion was not a meaningful measure of the effectiveness of Daylight Saving in the conservation of coal. But it did complicate debate on the issue. Thus, when Representative Charles Ellis Moore appeared before the committee, he announced that the opposition of truck farmers in Ohio was seconded by the Cambridge Collieries Company, operators of a dozen coal mines in his district. Another Ohio congressman, Roscoe McCulloch, seemed to be insulted on behalf of miners, mill workers, and marching bands in his district. "The laboring men who work in the shops, I believe are against this law," he broadly claimed with no more or less authority than anyone else who'd spoken that day. It was bad enough that workers in his district "have to get up, in fact, at 3:30 in the morning," McCulloch said, though neither he nor anyone else ventured to explain why Daylight Saving had apparently forced everyone in the Midwest to shop until eleven o'clock at night and tumble out of bed after four hours of sleep. The greater indignity? "We have to do it in order to protect the 'stupid' fellow in New York who does not want to get up in the morning according to the regular time."

On the floor of the House of Representatives, Daylight Saving had become a New York thing. And then the president of the National Daylight Saving Association, Marcus Marks, appeared before the House hearings committee. Marks resided at 200 Fifth Avenue in New York City. He was also president of the New York Daylight Saving Association, former borough president for Manhattan, and longtime leader of the Merchants' Association of New York. Asked to describe how New York had fared when the Standard Time zones had been drawn across the map of America, Marks blithely replied, "New York is practically on sun time," as if this were a matter of celestial justice. Presented with the concerns of farmers who felt displaced from sun time, Marks said, "We will adjust it with them," as if he were the nation's official timekeeper, adding, "for heaven's sake on account of a few farmers being inconvenienced, let us not disturb the whole country." Congressman Sanders of Indiana informed Marks that the United Mine Workers in his district were "solidly against" the law. "I wonder why," Marks replied, "for they work underground. I should not think getting up an hour earlier could possibly make any difference to them." When Sanders said that miners, like farmers, believed it would be "just as easy for people in New York City who want this change to get up an hour earlier," Marks imperiously declared, "It cannot be done."

After Marcus Marks left the House of Representatives, freshman Congressman James Strong asked his colleagues to remember what Marks had told them about the men who had delivered Daylight Saving to the nation.

> He spoke of the organization of his daylight association. He told you it was composed of all classes of people. He said they met at the Waldorf-Astoria in New York and organized their association. How many farmers and "real, honest-to-God working men" do you think were at that meeting who traveled from all over the United States and paid their railroad fares and were able to board and put up at that kind of a hotel? Who do you think organized it?

In the early summer of 1919, President Wilson returned from Versailles with an official declaration of peace, which endorsed his plan to establish the League of Nations. The U.S. Senate refused to ratify the league or the treaty. The Congress simply neglected its duty to make the peace official. But "in the stately chamber where he and his revered colleagues perform their momentous duties," the *New York Times* reported, Senator Williams of Mississippi "was heard with gravity and respect by his fellow law-makers. 'I am opposed,' he said, 'to Congress undertaking to usurp not only the powers of the Executive and the States, but those of God Almighty, and seeking to fix the time when the sun shall rise and set.'" The Congress was more committed to ending Daylight Saving than it was to the formal conclusion of a worldwide war.

Partisan and regional divisions had been scrambled by the Daylight Saving debate, as had the minds of almost everyone in the country. The Congressional Record on the topic reads like a transcript from the Tower of Babel. Even the simplest of propositions— Did the nation save coal during two seasons of Daylight Saving?—was unanswered after hundreds of hours of testimony, including a fantastic exchange between several congressmen and the soap-and-toothpaste magnate, Sidney M. Colgate, of Colgate & Company, forerunner of Colgate-Palmolive. For starters, Colgate introduced himself as a representative of "the International Daylight Saving Association, the New York Daylight Saving Association, the Merchants' Association of New York, and I was told by the president of the Daylight Saving Association that I might represent the State Federation of Women's Clubs."

Sidney Colgate represented everything but the facts. He raised the vital issue of fuel conservation in his introductory comments: "There is a vast saving in coal and wood, but that fact might go without question. There are hundreds of thousands and even millions of tons of coal saved annually by this daylight-saving bill."

Questioner: It does save a large amount of coal?

Colgate: Yes, sir; there is no question about that.

Q: Used in the manufacture of gas and electric light?

C: Yes, sir.

Q: Have you looked into that?

C: Well, it is a self evident fact, and there are some things we know, and that you know perfectly well, and yet we may not have exact figures on them. I know that in our house we light our electric lights an hour later than otherwise.

Q: Don't you light them an hour earlier in the morning?

C: Yes; but we do not get up that soon. I do not mean to say that because we are of the privileged class in our particular house, but I will guarantee that most of the people in the United States to-day do not get up before sunrise; they do not use electric lights in the morning at all, or at least very, very little in the summer time. It makes a vast difference in the evening, on the other hand.

Q: You spoke about coal. The time is changed during the summer months, but during the winter months it is with the sun, and how do you figure out the coal proposition then?

C: How do I figure it out?

Q: Yes.

C: Well, it leaves us as we were. Of course, we would save more coal probably if this daylight saving existed throughout the year. Don't you see it?

Q: That is what I say. . . . How do you figure out a saving of coal, then?

C: Well, there is a saving of coal in the summer time. Of course, not as much as in the winter . . .

Q: How do you save coal during the summer time?

C: Of course, you save it.

Q: How?

C: Well, take the city of Washington—.

Q: Do you save any more coal during the summer if the hour is changed than without its being changed?

C: If you start your light in Washington an hour later...

Q: Yes; but you are not burning electric light during the time this law is operative, as you have just told one of the members of this committee.

C: I am sorry that I am so dense that I can not understand that or can not explain this to the gentleman. I wish one of the members of the committee would explain it to him ...

Q: In the early months in the spring and the late months in the fall, when in fact you are burning a great deal of coal after dark, the manufacturers are ...

C: It does not do everything, and does not save all the coal in the country, but it saves quite a little. I know it was thought so, and that was not questioned at the time of the war, when we wanted to save coal. People thought we were saving coal at that time, and I am sure we were.

In late June 1919, with Daylight Saving still in effect, many Americans in the Midwest were marveling as twilight stretched itself toward 10 P.M. But a more "astonishing change in the daylight saving situation" was observed in New York. At the annual convention of the American Federation of Labor, the delegates voted 450 to 180 in favor of the repeal of Daylight Saving. When someone finally asked their opinion, the industrial workers had sided with the farmers. An incredulous *New York Times* editorialized, "But that the vote was a correct expression of organized labor's will, if not exactly unbelievable, at least need not be believed until better proof than this vote is given."

In July, Congress passed the agricultural appropriations bill with the rider repealing Daylight Saving. President Wilson vetoed it. An attempt to override his veto did not garner the necessary two-thirds to hold, so Congress passed a second law repealing Daylight. Wilson explained that he vetoed that bill "with the utmost reluctance . . . [but Daylight Saving] ministers to economy and to efficiency. And the interest of the farmer is not in all respects separated from these interests." A congressional vote to override the second presidential veto was expected on 20 August.

Congress had rarely asserted its will over two presidential vetoes, but most newspapers were betting that the farm team would defeat the city boys. The captain of the presumptive losers, the *New York Times,* had tossed in the towel weeks earlier, and with it went any veneer of objectivity in the newspaper's reporting on members of Congress:

> Another Wise One—Representative Campbell of Kansas—said that the law should be repealed because it took the farmers out into the fields while the dew was on them, and "everybody knows that when dew gets on the body it makes sores." After hearing, from such high sources, such statements as these, bold will be he who continues to express an affection for an added hour of day-lighted leisure. The mere fact that a great majority of the country's inhabitants want it is no reason why they should have it—can't be.

Congress overrode President Wilson's second veto by a vote of 223 to 101. The national Daylight Saving law was repealed by 116 Republicans and 107 Democrats. One hundred members of the House of Representatives had not voted on the veto override, which the *New York Times* bemoaned as "the supineness of the majority. When the crucial test came, our representatives were not there." As for the farmers, it must have seemed they got what they wanted that summer, but all they eventually got was the blame for Daylight Saving.

Chapter Three

Moon over Miami

As a rule, we disbelieve all facts and theories for which we have no use.

—WILLIAM JAMES, 1897

The weakness of moral reasoning is that it is usually irrational. The strength of moral reasoning is that most people are irrational.

The United States adopted Daylight Saving in 1918 because it was presented as a moral necessity. The mere possibility that the war effort might be better fueled and our soldiers better supplied had persuaded even farmers, who had "endured it while the war was going on because they thought it really was a war measure," explained Representative James Strong of Kansas. "Their boys had gone to France; they were willing to do anything." When the war ended, the supporters of Daylight Saving suddenly lost this moral high ground, and they had nothing comparable to stand on during the congressional debate that ensued. They had assembled no real evidence to substantiate the economic, social, or psychological benefits they attributed to the manipulation of the country's clocks. "As a matter of fact, the law was never necessary," gloated one of Daylight's opponents in a letter to the *New York Times* after the national legislation was repealed in August 1919. "We could have beaten Germany equally well without it."

Daylight Saving had not simply fallen from grace. According to its critics, it had nearly dragged the whole world to hell with it. "We can look forward to all the European nations abolishing this wickedness and awakening as it were out of a nightmare of a species of blasphemy akin to the worship of Baal," predicted one New Jersey reader of the *Times,* distancing himself from the Daylight idolaters in New York City and Berlin. "When the Germans began the curse of 'daylight saving,' they started on the course which ended in their great fall...they did not care for God or man." Within weeks of the repeal, city halls across the country were besieged by requests from citizens eager to turn their clocks back to God's time before the appointed Sunday in October. "God's time is true. Man-made time is false," declared Congressman E. S. Candler of Mississippi, fueling the hellfires. "Truth is always mighty and should prevail. God alone can create daylight."

God alone knows why the overwhelmingly Christian Congress had chosen Sunday as the day to begin and end Daylight Saving each year, but this choice occasioned a lot of sermonizing against the legislation from preachers who considered the choice of Sunday further proof of the godlessness of government. For many Americans who believed that time was the provenance of the divine, Daylight Saving represented an assault on the constitutional separation of church and state. One of these latter-day Jeffersonians lived in Oxford, New York. According to a fellow parishioner who documented the episode for the *New York Times,* he had forgotten to set his clock ahead on the last Sunday of April in 1918, and "entered the church door as the pastor pronounced the [closing] benediction." As luck, or the heavens, would have it, that first day of Daylight Saving in America was Easter Sunday. "'I'll never go to church again,' he declared when the situation was explained, 'until daylight saving is abolished and we go back to God's time.'"

God is famously inscrutable, and efforts to divine the Almighty's timekeeping preferences have resulted in some impressive complications. Although Easter in 1918 fell on 31 March, Easter Sunday in 1919 was 20 April, and in 1920 it was 4 April. The arcane rules for identifying which Sunday will be Easter Sunday begin with the divination of the first Sunday after the first ecclesiastical full moon (distinct from the astronomical full moon) that occurs on or after the vernal equinox—and this calculus only applies to Catholics and Protestants. Eastern Orthodox Christians have another method entirely and, typically, designate a different Sunday as Easter. Moreover, the year 1919 was 5679 according to the Jewish calendar, and 1337 on the Islamic calendar. Given these discrepancies, how sincere was the invocation of God's time in relation to a single hour?

It was persistent. And it was not confined to pulpits or the right wing of Congress. According to the Washington Diarist for *The New Republic,* Daylight Saving Time was "distinct from natural time, which the Good Lord gave us on the first day, as is concisely reported in Genesis." This was the argument in 1919; but it was still the argument seventy years later, when the Washington Diarist published this diatribe against Daylight Saving in 1989: "What is day and what is night were clearly determined on the first day: 'And God called the light day, and darkness night,'" he continued. "Night falls, our language tells us. Let it fall when God and the sun ordain."

The God of Genesis not only sorted out night and day. He invented the week, a seven-day cycle without any astronomical significance, our only temporal unit that bears no relationship to the arrangement or operation of the sun, the earth, our moon, or any other heavenly sphere. God made it up. This innovative system of accrual relies on the ability of timekeepers to count the days, because one Sunday is otherwise indistinguishable from another Sunday or even a Friday. Sunrise effectively defines the beginning of a new day, and sunset heralds the arrival of each night. Unfortunately, God did not tell anyone exactly what time it was when darkness falls.

On 20 December 1919, with all the clocks in the country running on Standard Time, the sun set in Bangor, Maine, at 3:56 P.M. The sun would not set in New York City for another thirty-five minutes. So, at what time did night fall? What did four o'clock mean? In Miami, where clocks were synchronized with clocks in Bangor and New York—they are all in the same Eastern Standard Time Zone— the sun did not set until 5:34 P.M. Was four o'clock ordained day or night by God?

It got worse. Looking forward to the next year's summer solstice without Daylight Saving Time, residents of cities in the north could see they were in for a rude awakening. With no adjustment of the clocks, the sun would rise over the good people of Bangor at 3:49 A.M. on 20 June. What in God's name were they supposed to do in Bangor until their factories and offices opened four or five hours later? The official start of the day in New York would occur at 4:24 A.M., leaving the dilettantes and duffers plenty of time before work to take in a play or to play a round of golf—if someone could rouse the actors and caddies. In Miami, on 20 June, the sun would not rise until 5:30 A.M. For more than an hour and a half, according to God's time, day was night in Miami. These inconsistencies not only cast a shadow on scriptural time management. They also raised a serious question about the repeal of Daylight Saving. If Florida's farmers were expected to supply neighboring stores and schools with milk and produce in 1920 operating under the 5:30 sunrise ordained by God, why had farmers in New York been unable to do the same in 1919, when Daylight Saving Time had delayed sunrise time for them until 5:24?

Chapter Four

Banking on the Big Apple

Keep your splendid silent sun . . .
Keep your fields of clover and timothy, and your corn . . .
give me the streets of Manhattan!
—WALT WHITMAN, 1881

In the late spring of 1919, in a last-ditch effort to preserve the federal Daylight Saving law, the attorney general of New
York presented the United States Congress with a litany of local and
state ordinances, all of which anticipated the return of national Daylight Saving in April 1920. "Contracts great and small are governed by
it; banking transportation, navigation, traffic in liquors and food-
stuffs, Sunday observance, elections and court procedures are all
regulated by it," he wrote. "If there is a lack of conformity in State
and Federal statutes, vital rights might be involved."

Uniformity had been the logic of the federal legislation. Marcus
Marks, president of the National Daylight Saving Association, highlighted this reasoning during his testimony before the House of Representatives. Asked about the possibility of a compromise—restoring
the farmers to sun time, and allowing New Yorkers to turn their
clocks ahead—Marks said, "You cannot have these blessings by leg-

islation unless you have it by means of yourself and your neighbor operating under the same law." It was all or nothing, and in August 1919, Congress gave the New Yorkers nothing.

A few weeks later, Senator William Calder of New York, author of the federal Daylight Saving law, learned that the New York City Board of Aldermen was debating a proposal to institute local Daylight Saving in New York City. True to the principle of uniformity, Calder urged the aldermen not to pass a local ordinance. Like the attorney general, Calder foresaw "that the confusion would provoke much litigation and endless difficulty." Calder was in powerful company. The Western Union telegraph company, the International Mercantile Marine, and the owners and operators of every major freight and passenger railroad line in the country joined the chorus, warning of dire economic and practical consequences if individual cities attempted to exercise the local option and run their clocks ahead of Standard Time during the summer months.

"In the minds of the timorous, some apprehension may arise of inconveniences more or less serious if New York's clocks should be out of harmony with those in the rest of the country," admitted the *New York Times,* which was editorializing daily for passage of the local ordinance. But most cities "would soon find it next to necessary, and certainly judicious, to make their clocks agree with ours."

New York City was not alone in its desire for Daylight, but New York City was singular. By 1920, its population of 5.6 million was more than twice as big as Chicago's and three times as big as Philadelphia's, and over the next two decades, New York grew much faster than the nation's second- and third-largest cities, and five times faster than Boston, Providence, New Haven, and Baltimore. And it was not just big. New York was capacious. Within the boundaries of Manhattan, neighborhoods and city blocks from Harlem to Broadway to Fifth Avenue to Wall Street had themselves become world-renowned cultural and commercial capitals. New York City was indisputably the financial headquarters of the country, and in the aftermath of the war, it surpassed Paris and rivaled London as the capital of capital in the world.

"New York [was] merely one of the fruits of that great tree whose roots go down in the Mississippi Valley, and whose branches spread from one ocean to another," wrote Edward Martin in *The Wayfarer in New York* in 1909. But, echoing a complaint he'd heard from many midwesterners, he added, "the big apple gets a disproportionate share of the national sap." This first documented use of the city's nickname did not catch on. But the idea was in the air, and it soon became a commonplace. John J. Fitz Gerald, a sportswriter for the *New York Morning Telegraph,* was visiting a New Orleans racetrack in 1920, and he overheard an African-American stable hand say that he and the horse he was walking were headed for the Big Apple. Fitz Gerald, who is credited with popularizing the city's sobriquet in his column, knew immediately where they were headed. "There is only one Big Apple," he wrote. "That's New York."

In late September 1919, the president of the New York City Board of Aldermen declared, "Congress slipped something over on New York City and the country which the people did not want." He wanted Daylight in New York. The first endorsement of his proposed city ordinance came from the Merchants' Association of New York. And despite his earlier demand for a uniform, nationwide Daylight Saving policy, Marcus Marks gave the aldermen's local plan his emphatic approval. Marks and his National Daylight Saving Association shrugged off charges of hypocrisy and provincialism. New York, Marks asserted, was not going it alone; it was leading the nation. In the autumn of 1919, this was hubris; in December, it was still hubris, but Marks had stuck a feather in it. He told the *New York Times* that the Pennsylvania Railroad Company had decided to alter its timetables to serve New York City. The nation's largest rail operator conceded that "it would be impracticable to provide train service, especially for commutation travel, based on two standards of time." If a Daylight plan was adopted by "New York and other important cities," the railroad explained, "it will necessarily follow that the standard time of those cities shall be the standard time of the surrounding territory."

Labor leaders, banks, chambers of commerce, and hundreds of small businesses rallied behind the New York aldermen and their president, who didn't name names but hinted at even more powerful allies when he confided to the press that leading stock exchange firms had privately pledged their support. The aldermen's proposal was immediately signed into law by the mayor. Some observers considered the ordinance redundant because the entire state of New York would be governed by a Daylight Saving law in 1920. But similar laws in every other state in the union had been repealed or allowed to expire, and New York City wasn't counting on any favors from the farmers, who were already complaining that the statewide Daylight law had cost them more than $10 million in agricultural output.

If there was room to doubt the accuracy of the farmers' math and to question their devotion to God's time, surely there was reason to wonder why New York City was hell-bent on having its summer sunsets delayed. The previous winter should have been on the minds of many of them. The *New York Times* had documented the "double menace of zero weather and delayed fuel shipments" due to the national coal shortage, and the lingering "fear of empty coal bunkers, collapse of elevator service, [and] suspension of building operation," which justified drastic conservation methods. The nation had not addressed its systemic fuel-consumption problems by the time New York and other northeastern cities were facing the winter of 1919. And this was not strictly a seasonal or a regional concern. Reading lamps, stoves, hallway lights, hot water, and elevators all operated in the summer. Tall office buildings and high-rise apartments in every

American city relied on electric-fan ventilation systems, and the pressure for plumbing was provided by electric pumps. "The greatest industrial crime of the present generation has been the unrecoverable waste of America's fuel energy," declared the *Saturday Evening Post*. Yet public officials in New York and elsewhere could not sell Daylight Saving to the public as a conservation measure.

The District of Columbia was hit hard by the ongoing national coal shortage in December 1919. "Curtailment of passenger service on railroads entering Washington was announced by the United States railroad administration," announced the *Washington Post*. The Pennsylvania Railroad's "Broadway Limited" run to New York was withdrawn, as were trains to Pittsburgh and points west and all excursions and specials on the Baltimore & Ohio tracks. A comprehensive, two-thousand-word advisory, "How Washingtonians May Reduce Their Coal Bills," was published in the *Post*. No mention was made of Daylight Saving as a conservation scheme. Instead, the analysis culminated in an unwittingly poignant practical recommendation:

> The excessive temperature we require in our houses and offices is to a great extent psychological, and the thermometer has a lot to do with this condition, because how frequently we have no feeling of cold until we look at the thermometer and find that it registers a temperature below seventy, then we are suddenly taken with a chill and call frantically for more heat. If all the thermometers in the United States could be changed so that when the temperature is 65 degrees Fahrenheit they would register 70 degrees Fahrenheit, there would be little complaint and we would save 27,976,241 tons of coal each year.

Three years earlier, in an effort to discredit Daylight Saving, this same scheme had been proposed to the British Parliament by the Royal Astronomer as a practical joke.

Fuel economy, the principal justification for Daylight Saving during World War I, simply did not figure in the critical New York City debate. By 1920, saving fuel had fallen to sixth place on the top-ten list of rationales published by the Merchants' Association, below "relief of eyestrain."

One reason was the unreliability of the data. Estimates for fuel saving continued to vary as wildly as the estimates of farm losses. Had Daylight Saving saved the nation $4, $6, $8, or $10 million in annual gas and electric light use? Had Americans conserved 1, 1.5, or 2 million tons of coal? Even today, the best evidence of fuel saving has to be inferred. As early as 1916, the *New York Times* reported that the "illuminating industry" in Germany had petitioned the government "to abolish daylight saving as soon as possible, as the new order of things is playing havoc with the thousands dependent upon the old-time lavish consumption of paraffin, gas, and electricity." In 1917, the New York Edison Company predicted that Daylight Saving would have "a serious effect upon our business. . . . The situation as to coal and labor is disconcerting. It is impossible to make any coal contracts." In 1919, Marcus Marks claimed he had "received information that, although the sentiment against the law seems to come from farmers, it is really fostered by the large gas companies." *Times* editorials hinted several times in 1919 and 1920 about "secret exaggerators and manipulators of the rustic grievance," but evidence of this conspiracy was never discovered.

"The whole thing is pure humbug," declared one Michigan reader of *Scientific American* in the autumn of 1919. (His letter had been withheld from publication along with many others, the editors of the magazine admitted. "We have been living in hope that enough of our subscribers would support daylight saving to make the thing more of a discussion." This letter from Michigan, along with a number of other scientific objections from across the country, was finally published a few months after the repeal of the national legislation.) "Do you know how the city man spends his extra hour in the evening? He cranks up his car and goes out into the country for a spin." The writer figured this negated any fuel saving claimed for the Daylight scheme, and, he added, "gasoline resources are in a good deal worse shape than coal."

The *New York Times* sounded sanguine about the ways New Yorkers might spend or squander their extra hour, "for here, as nowhere else, are interests diversified. . . . What New York wants and intends to have must be what labor, commerce, and even leisure want." The editor of the *American Agriculturalist* took up this theme, embellished it, and turned it on the supporters of Daylight Saving, alleging that "'gasoline interests and the amusement people' were behind the mass of propaganda sent out" around New York to extend the statewide law beyond 1920.

Automobile production had boomed in the postwar economy, and cars complicated the Daylight debate. They split the interests of the nation's fuel suppliers. Unlike the coal and electricity producers, the petroleum industry became an ardent and often generous supporter of Daylight Saving because later sunset times seemed to encourage pleasure driving—and gasoline consumption.

As the farm lobby correctly alleged, manufacturers and entrepreneurs in the sports and recreation industries had benefited by Daylight Saving. But the "amusement people" were not all amused. Daylight Saving had seriously cut into Broadway theater receipts. Darkness did not arrive on Broadway until after the curtains went up, complained the playwright responsible for the farce *Nightie Night*. Concert halls and opera houses also reported drops in attendance after the clocks were advanced. With more than 250 plays in production each year, the New York theatrical community was a legitimate economic force. To express its disapproval of the city's ordinance, the International Theatrical Association passed a somewhat melodramatic resolution against the time change, "taking the stand that the law is not only inimical to the theatre interests but also to the interests of all citizens of the United States." Why didn't the Board of Aldermen respond to these overtures?

Even more powerful were the owners of the nation's movie theaters. They shared Broadway's complaints, but they were backed by bigger numbers. In 1922, the movie industry reported 40 million paid admissions per week; by 1929, weekly movie admissions topped 100 million. In 1930, when a statewide Daylight Saving referendum appeared on the ballot in California, the record-breaking $200,000 campaign to defeat it was financed by "the movie industry and the utilities, fearful of losing business, with the active support of clergy, Protestant and Catholic, who anticipated declines in summer church attendance," according to an analysis in the *American Political Science Review*. As early as 1921, there were already ten thousand movie theaters in the United States—and Times Square in New York had more than its share. The movie theater owners held their annual convention in New Jersey that year, and they called for an end to Daylight Saving, but New York City ignored them.

The Big Apple had taken a shine to Daylight Saving. If this hadn't happened, residents of North America would have been permanently spared the annual stem-winding ritual and its attendant controversies. Congress had flatly rejected Daylight Saving, as had lawmakers in every statehouse outside New York. In cities across the country, the few elected officials who mourned the loss of extended summer evenings were wary of exercising the local option, which would put them out of sync with their suburban neighbors. In 1919, Canada rescinded its national Daylight Saving law. Mexico had resisted the idea from the start. By 1920, the federal, state, provincial, and county governments throughout North America had disavowed and discontinued the practice of Daylight Saving. And yet, year after year, Americans are told, as they were told by *The New Republic* in 1989, "the history of daylight-saving time is a textbook example of our tolerance of meddling by government in what is none of its business."

More than a few people were meddling with time in New York, but they didn't work for the government. There was a word for what they were doing, and it began with the letter *A*, but it was not *apple*. The word on the street in New York was *arbitrage*.

When the clocks in England first leaped ahead in 1917, the board of managers of the New York Cotton Exchange immediately urged passage of a Daylight Saving law, explaining to the *New York Times* that it "would lead to an increased opportunity for arbitrage." In fact, without Daylight Saving, the commodities, stock, and bond traders on Wall Street could expect no opportunity at all for arbitrage—buying securities on one market for immediate resale in another market at an advantageous price and profiting by the price discrepancy. That is, easy money. These price differences are typically brief—often momentary. And in a market of constantly changing valuations—the Twenties was a decade of unprecedented speculation on Wall Street—even tiny differences in stock prices could be leveraged into big profits. Currency trading offered similar opportunities.

Trading on the London Stock Exchange ended daily at 3 P.M., as did trading on the mercantile exchanges in Liverpool. Trading on the New York Stock Exchange began at 9 A.M., the established opening hour for stock exchanges throughout the United States and for most banks and commercial institutions. Standard Time had established a five-hour difference between London and New York. When it was 9 A.M. in New York, it was 2 P.M. in London. This preserved one hour of the trading day for arbitrage. Then London shoved ahead its clocks by an hour in 1917, and when the New York Exchange opened at 9 A.M., it was 3 P.M. and closing time in London.

Daylight Saving saved New York's most precious hour.

Money makes men bold. On 25 March 1920, the stock exchanges in Boston and Philadelphia announced their intention to conform to the Daylight Saving hours set by New York. The *New York Times* tracked the domino effect across the country. On the same day, Cleveland's traders became Daylight Savers, even though "clocks in the Cleveland Stock Exchange will be the only time pieces [in the city] to move one hour ahead." And before night fell on Chicago, which was in the Central Time Zone and normally one hour behind New York, the board of governors of the exchange "voted to fix the hours of trading from 8 A.M. to I P.M. . . . until such time as a daylight saving law may be adopted here." One week later, all the banks in Chicago opted to open early rather than lag two hours behind the Big Apple, as "business under this condition is impossible."

In June 1920, the Chicago City Council passed a Daylight Saving ordinance. That autumn, after Chicago's clocks had been turned back to Central Standard Time, Sam Cardinella was convicted of murdering another resident of the Windy City and sentenced to die on 15 April 1921. Cardinella's fate generated a lot of newspaper copy before and after his execution. His fellow gang members had allegedly convinced him to go on a hunger strike in prison, and Cardinella reportedly lost more than fifty pounds—not as a matter of principle, but as a matter of gravity. His former associates figured he wouldn't die if he was hanged as a bantamweight, and they could claim his limp body from the gallows and resuscitate him. Instead, on the big day, Sam fainted, an ignominy Ernest Hemingway exaggerated for a chapter of *In Our Time,* in which Sam Cardinella soils himself as the noose is lowered around his neck and wins a rebuke from the chaplain for his unmanly performance. But in the Big Apple, the real moral of Sam's story was reported by the *New York Times.* On Wednesday morning, 13 April, Sam woke up with a question.

"When am I going to be hanged?" he asked Assistant Jailer Lorenz Moistenheim.
"Friday morning at 8 o'clock," said Mr. Moistenheim.
"Central, standard, or Chicago time?"

"Chicago time," replied Mr. Moistenheim. "It's in Chicago you're going to be hanged."

"Yes," said Cardinella, "but I was sentenced before the time was changed. This rearrangement deprives me of an hour of life. That won't mean anything after I'm dead, but it will mean a lot on Friday morning. The Governor can change his mind in that time."

Jail officials changed the hanging time to 9 o'clock Chicago time.

There were some New Yorkers who actually grew apples. And what the hardworking farmers and hardscrabble rural communities of New York State wanted in 1920 was relief. Travel and trade were complicated by the time difference with communities in neighboring states, according to representatives of the grange, the Farm Bureau, and the Dairymen's Association, all of which were lobbying the legislature in Albany for repeal. They estimated that the confusion had increased farmers' costs by 10 to 25 percent and seriously limited their productivity. Suffering under the last statewide Daylight Saving law in the country had not improved the moods of New York's farmers. They predicted that New York's milk supply would dry up by mid-August, the price of eggs would rise to three dollars a dozen, and—stopping just shy of calling for a plague of frogs upon Manhattan—the farmers prophesied to the governor and the *New York Times* that "New York State faces a food famine during which the 'farmer will look after himself first and let the city people wait.'"

It was February 1921. The fate of the statewide law was obvious to everyone in Albany. Unless the heavens opened up and sent forth a messenger to inform lawmakers that God had switched sides, the statewide Daylight Saving law was doomed.

Enter Royal S. Copeland, New York City commissioner of health, bearing typhus, smallpox, tuberculosis, bubonic plague, and "one hundred and thirty-three thousand babies."

One hundred and thirty-three thousand babies born in New York last year. You put these little shavers shoulder to shoulder and they would reach twenty-two miles. Some babies! Were they born on Fifth Avenue and Riverside Drive and Central Park West and the Park Slope in Brooklyn? They were not. Over one hundred thousand of these babies were born in the tenements of New York. . . . You multiply that by ten years and you have a million. . . . I wouldn't want to take the responsibility of walking up to the Great White Throne someday and being asked, 'Did you do anything which resulted in infant deaths in New York?' . . . [T]he responsibility will be yours, and I don't propose to carry it. We have here in this hour of sunlight one of the best possible means of raising resistance for the human body and . . . preventing these ravaging diseases. No matter what your platform might have said on Daylight Saving, you cannot afford to look your constituents in the face and say: I voted for a repeal of a measure which has in it such a large degree of health precaution as this law has. . . . I know the heart of the country people as well as you do; I was born on a farm. I expect to die on a farm. I know how they feel. And when they realize that the health of the children and of the mothers and of all the boys and girls of New York City depends upon having all the sunlight and fresh air they can get, so to be taken out of these miserable tenements where they live without light or ventilation, I know they will excuse you if you change the platform you were elected upon.

Royal Copeland's speech was a genuine barn burner. And in the light of his righteous passion, anyone with eyes could see that Daylight Saving was on the side of the angels. Dr. Copeland was rewarded with a seat in the U.S. Senate in 1922, and he served there until his death in 1938.

The farmers were not moved, however. They had babies of their own, they said, and they could barely feed them. The assemblymen repealed the New York State Daylight Saving law. In 1921, all that was standing between New York City and darkness was a local ordinance. But New York was not alone.

In the spring of 1921, the *Washington Post* reported, Daylight Saving would be in effect "in most of the large cities and industrial centers in the northern section of the Eastern time zone, in the majority of the larger cities in the Northeastern section of the central time zone, but, as far as reports are obtainable, will not be put into effect in the Southern or Western states." Some Americans called this progress; others called it the disintegration of Standard Time; everyone was calling on the federal government to intercede. "The lesson of the whole business," declared the *North American Review* in June 1921, "obviously is that Congress should exercise its Constitutional power, and perform its Constitutional duty, of prescribing uniform time-measurements and reckonings for the whole country."

The worldwide organizing principle of time zones and the literal meaning of Standard Time were all but lost in America. At the annual meeting of the Governing Committee of the New York Stock Exchange in April 1921, the members resolved to open and close the exchange according to the absolutely nonstandard "standard New York City time." This sort of talk put New Jersey in "an unenviable position," the *New York Times* graciously acknowledged. The New Jersey State Senate had rejected a Daylight Saving bill. This left thousands of residents "in a badly tangled state of affairs [where] it will be possible for a commuter living forty-five minutes from New York City to reach his home fifteen minutes before he started." By the summer of 1921, "virtually all cities and industrial towns" in the Garden State had passed local ordinances to keep time with New York City.

Hartford followed suit, though most of the rest of Connecticut did not. Thus, in April 1921, the elected members of the Connecticut Assembly were unwittingly deposited in Hartford one hour before the appointed opening of their legislative session, because the timetables of the New York, New Haven, and Hartford Railroad had been altered to conform to New York City time. As a result, lawmakers from across the state had an hour to kill on benches in Bushnell Park, reported the *New York Times,* so they "discussed measures of punishment for Hartford." In May, they proposed a twenty-five-dollar fine for "officials who countenance daylight saving, and the same penalty on all persons doing business with the public and displaying clocks which are not an hour behind daylight-saving time." Two years later, the renegade state capital had not stopped messing with its clocks, so the assemblymen upped the ante. They passed a new law, which stipulated "that the public display of a timepiece running on other than standard time, including wrist watches and street and store clocks, shall be illegal." Violators faced fines of up to one hundred dollars, or up to ten days in prison, or both.

As Congress had isolated New York City in the national Daylight Saving debate and set it up as the opponent of farmer and factory workers, so cities across the northern United States began to single themselves out from their appointed states, organizing themselves into an unofficial metropolitan league. Several state legislatures attempted to curtail the growing independence of their principal cities. In the Far North, lawmakers in New Hampshire were so impressed by the Connecticut fine that they soon crafted a bill prohibiting Daylight Saving anywhere in the state; violators faced a five-hundred-dollar fine. No single city in New Hampshire possessed the economic clout or a population sufficient to sustain independence on the time issue. But this did not spare the state the ravages of Daylight Saving Time. Although it was not a state of commuters, New Hampshire enjoyed a geographic and economic situation almost as unenviable as New Jersey's. The entire Granite State was basically a whistle-stop on the Boston and Maine Railroad's run between Boston and Bangor after the railroad revised its timetables to conform to the clocks in Boston. Passenger and freight trains blew through New Hampshire an hour sooner than anticipated, and they didn't stop to pay a fine.

Boston had not merely followed New York's lead. In 1921, Boston had railroaded through the Massachusetts legislature the only statewide Daylight Saving law in the nation. It was this law that Bay State farmers blamed for millions in annual losses, and their complaint became the basis for the state grange's appeal to the U.S. Supreme Court. For several years, the National Grange had been angling for this fight. At its 1923 convention in Pittsburgh, the grange had elected "masters" from ten northeastern states to agitate against existing Daylight Saving laws, according to the *New York Times*. The masters were instructed "to set on foot a campaign for the passage of a new 'Standard Time' law, so worded that it will be a Federal statute with which the individual States cannot interfere." In 1926, the test case made it to the U.S. Supreme Court. The Court ruled against the grange. Dismissing the proposition that Massachusetts farmers were owed compensation for damages allegedly suffered as the result of the state's Daylight law, the Court articulated the principles and precedents that put Daylight Saving legislation well within the purview of any state legislature. The Supreme Court's majority opinion was delivered by Justice Oliver Wendell Holmes, a native of Boston.

"The usual chaos of 'standard time' and 'daylight saving time' again prevails in America," complained the *North American Review* in the summer of 1928, "and will probably recur every year, until Congress summons up sufficient gumption to perform its Constitutional duty and put an end to the foolishness." By the spring of the following year, more than 25 million Americans in sixteen states were observing Daylight Saving. Most of the participating cities and towns had adopted an abbreviated five-month schedule (the last Sunday in April through the last Sunday in September), but there was no end to the variations. Rutland, Vermont, waited until the last Sunday in May to advance its clocks, and Auburn, Maine, invented a three-month period, from mid-June through mid-September. But the Massachusetts law remained an anomaly; in ten years, no city, and no aggregation of cities and towns within another state, had converted metropolitan support into a statewide law.

This reluctance made sense in rural Vermont—Bennington was the first Vermont town to adopt postwar Daylight Saving, and it waited until 1928; and it made sense in Delaware, Wisconsin, and other states where very few localities participated in the clock change. Minnesota, for instance, was included in the optimistic annual roundup of Daylight Saving states compiled by the Merchants' Association of New York, though the fine print revealed that only "members of the Minneapolis Chamber of Commerce observe daylight saving." Indiana, a state famous for its schismatic approach to Daylight Saving, launched its ambivalent history in 1928 in Indianapolis. The city council passed a Daylight Saving ordinance, the mayor nixed it, the council overrode his veto, the banks and most retail stores observed the time change, the public schools ignored it, and roughly half of the city's manufacturing plants went one way or the other.

Anomalies were the rule. Michigan in general and Detroit in particular had been recalibrating their clocks for so long and in such inventive ways that no one in the country really knew what time it was in those famous Ford automobile factories. In any given year, in published newspaper and magazine tallies, Detroit was counted as a Central Time Zone city observing Daylight Saving; a Central Time Zone city experimenting with Eastern Time; or, an Eastern Time Zone city not observing Daylight Saving. All were ultimately incorrect; all were behind Detroit time by at least an hour. The Motor City gradually transformed itself into an Eastern Time Zone city observing Daylight Saving, a feat that accounted for its fantastically late summer sunsets. In June, civil twilight in Detroit—the hours during which no artificial illumination was needed for outdoor activity—extended from 5:20 A.M. till almost 10 P.M.

Elsewhere, the failure of cities to cultivate statewide legislation during the 1920s defied numerical and political logic. In Rhode Island, 75 percent of the population was practicing Daylight Saving by 1920, but their elected officials did not deliver a statewide law during the next ten years. Neither were Maine legislators persuaded, though Portland, Lewiston, and Bangor all sprang ahead, not to mention half of Biddeford, where industrial workers observed Daylight Saving but school and municipal officials did not. Pittsburgh and Philadelphia, their suburbs, and at least eight other large Pennsylvania towns advanced their clocks, but the state assembly didn't take the leap. Wilmington, Delaware; Chicago, Illinois; Toledo, Columbus, Dayton, Cincinnati, and a host of smaller cities in Ohio; even the Big Apple, the beacon for 25 million American Daylighters, could not make state lawmakers see the light.

In October 1929, a month after those observant cities turned their clocks back to Standard Time, the stock market crashed. Black Thursday took the shine off Wall Street for a while. But there was a strange new light on the horizon. Before the Depression set in, the *Washington Post* reported that "efforts to induce hens to lay more eggs by artificially prolonging 'daylight' . . . [have] increased the winter's yield of eggs five-fold on an experimental farm." It was, according to the *Post*, "but one of the ways in which electricity is being utilized by the farmer to increase his income and shorten his working day."

Chapter Five

Capitol Sports

Cultivated leisure is the aim of man.
—OSCAR WILDE, 1890

There is nary a professional or an amateur sport in the United States without its Hall of Fame. And yet not one of these American Valhallas has enshrined the name of any of the men who contributed an hour to every afternoon of the outdoor sports season. Instead, Daylight Saving is remembered as an austerity measure.

This is largely the fault of Daylight's most ardent proponents. Memorably portrayed by Republican Congressman James Strong of Kansas as "swivel-chair ornaments" seeking to indulge their slothful, sun-worshipping habits at the expense of hardworking men in the factories and fields, Daylight advocates turned themselves into neo-Puritans, self-appointed conservators of the nation's resources. It didn't make them popular; moreover, it cast a permanent shadow on Daylight Saving, which most Americans still see as the mark of the hulking federal bureaucracy, a dark and vast presence encroaching upon their private concerns.

The principal public proponents of Daylight Saving were, in fact, rather like the men their opponents accused them of being. They were wealthy professionals and middle-class merchants, they enjoyed their leisure, and they all had a big soft spot for the sun. Daylight Saving appealed to them precisely because it accommodated their habits and hobbies. Like the vast majority of their fellow citizens, they preferred an afternoon in the park to an afternoon in the mines. What they were proposing with the reapportionment of available summer sunshine was not a saving scheme; for reasons noble and not so, they were proposing National Time Out. But they lacked the courage of their secular convictions.

Most Americans don't associate any name—not even Ben Franklin—with Daylight Saving. Indeed, they don't attach much to it at all except an *s*, pluralizing the word *savings*. This gratuitous *s* serves no grammatical purpose. The illogic of this false plural pleased Daylight's critics; it was evidence that the scheme was riddled with falsehoods. They took to calling it Daylight Wasting Time—never *wastings*. But what's in a name? As editorialists and schoolkids have been reminding us for more than one hundred years, Daylight Saving doesn't actually produce any savings.

It did produce a lot of good sports. This should have made Daylight Saving enormously popular with the American public. But the scheme had been presented to the nation as a battle plan, so it was impossible for the Wilson White House to exploit the sports angle without looking like hypocrites.

This benefit was immediately apparent to other residents of the nation's capital. "If the government had especially desired to do something to foster and promote golf, it could not have made a better move than to turn the clock ahead," opined *Washington Post* sportswriter Francis Ouimet in May 1918.

Secretaries of many clubs I have been in touch with are preparing for the greatest response to golf that the country has ever seen, and this despite the fact that owing to the war very few tournaments will be played this year. With the additional hour of daylight, it will be possible to play until 9'clock, especially if one has a sharp-eyed caddie. And during the months of June and July, when the daylight lingers longest, one might stay on the links until 9:30. This means that a man may leave his place of business as late as 4:30 or even 5 o'clock, and allowing an hour in which to reach his particular course, he will still have time to play eighteen holes before darkness descends on him.

The first time the clocks were changed, school and neighborhood leagues in New England staged twilight track-and-field meets, racetracks in New York delayed the start of their afternoon races to attract more patrons to the betting booths, and the membership of the United States National Lawn Tennis Association unanimously endorsed the salutary effects of Daylight Saving on its programs and tournament attendance. Even at Princeton, where Woodrow Wilson had made his national reputation as an Ivy League president, the athletic option was exercised. "By taking advantage of the daylight saving, the Princeton oarsmen have been able to assemble the entire eight at the same time," reported the *New York Times* in 1918. "They are holding their practice from 6 to 7 in the evening after military work is finished for the day."

Instead of taking credit for the most popular government giveaway in history, the Wilson White House turned itself into a symbol of sacrifice, determined to put the saving back in Daylight. Lillian Rogers Parks, a White House seamstress and maid during World War I, remembered the "meatless days, heatless days, Sunday gasless days, meaning no Sunday pleasure drives," and other economies practiced at the urging of Woodrow Wilson. "Conservation was the byword around the White House; eight sheep were soon gracing the lawns," Parks recalled, adding, "many thousands of dollars were raised for the Red Cross through the auctioning of wool."

At best, Woodrow Wilson was a symbolic shepherd; at worst, he was a duffer in sheep's clothing. He was a genuinely fanatic golfer. During his eight years in office, he found time to play golf almost daily, and he dismissed reporters' questions about the amount of time he dedicated to the game. He was frequently spotted in midwinter, hitting black-painted golf balls in the snow. As *Golf Magazine* gleefully recounted, when the Germans sank the *Lusitania* in 1915, President Wilson had to be tracked down on a golf course, and the day after he submitted his formal request for a declaration of war to the Congress, he headed off to play golf at his private country club. Yet he failed to cultivate the support of this natural constituency and Daylight's greatest beneficiaries—the golfers and other athletes and fans whose numbers were multiplying exponentially.

During the 1920s, the last vestiges of golf's image as the sport of old men and socialites was erased by a string of victories posted in major tournaments by working-class amateurs and weekend golfers, including the great Bobby Jones. An amateur who retired from competition at twenty-eight, Jones is still the only golfer in history to win the Grand Slam—all four major American and British championships—in a single year. As the British commentator Alistair Cooke recalled in a *Letter from America* broadcast by the BBC, "Bobby Jones inspired a new national fad. One day, a young reporter walked into the *Baltimore Sun* office wearing plus fours and carrying a golf bag. [H. L.] Mencken was appalled at the costume.... He sat down and wrote an indignant column, which ended: 'If I had my way, any man guilty of golf would be ineligible for any office of trust under these United States.'"

At least one golfer was unhappy with Daylight Saving. He complained to the *New York Times* about his problems on the links. "Before the daylight saving law went into effect, I sometimes got as far as 250 yards on my drives, owing to the roll of the ball. This year, my drives land dead, the wet grass holding the ball, and my scores have been miserable. The dew on the grass is responsible." A Connecticut golfer advised him to equip his caddie with a big roll of blotting paper, or else adopt the habit of golfing in the afternoon and then retreating to the nineteenth hole to regale other golfers with "the stroke by stroke history of his game.... The memory of a faulty stroke is, like the dew, soon eradicated by the blessed sunlight."

In 1921, the *Times* calculated that Iowa, "a typical corn and hog state," had as many golf courses per capita as New York did, "and links in the West are being laid out faster than in the East." This was the first major wave of golf-course construction in the United States, and it lasted until the Depression. Someone in the Daylight movement should have seen it coming. As the *Washington Post* reported, an industrial statistician had calculated that golf ball sales in the first nine months of 1918—the first year of Daylight Saving—totaled $10.5 million, an increase of nearly 20 percent over sales for the entire previous year.

If Wilson and his fellow Democrats adopted a hypocritically and self-defeating abstemious public posture to promote Daylight Saving, their unsportsmanlike conduct was equaled by the Republicans, who shamelessly courted the farm vote and portrayed the federal law as a hoax. For two summers, according to Republicans in Congress, the nation had been forced to swallow Daylight Saving as a wartime prescription for conservation, health, and efficiency. By the fall of 1919, coal and gasoline supplies were short, milk and eggs were more expensive than ever, and influenza, polio, and tuberculosis were ravaging the nation. The persistence of these shortages and scourges, despite Daylight Saving, made Americans feel like fools; at the behest of their government, they'd been drinking snake oil. And for what? "In order to let fellows get away an extra hour to play golf," declared Congressman Strong, echoing a charge made by legislators from across the country.

In July 1921, when these indignant congressmen finally passed a joint declaration ending World War I—which had actually ended more than two years earlier—they had to locate Warren G. Harding, the Republican who succeeded Woodrow Wilson, to secure his signature. The White House attaché was dispatched to New Jersey, where he waited until late afternoon. President Harding turned up "wearing a Palm Beach suit, white shoes, white socks with black clocks, a white shirt buttoned by removable gold studs, and a green and red bow tie," according to the sartorially alert reporter for the *New York Times*. Harding had just finished a round of eighteen at the Somerset Hills Country Club. This was not an unusual day. During his first term, Harding had removed Wilson's symbolic sheep from the White House lawn and, according to the *Woman Citizen*, "President Harding takes off his office coat about sunset every evening and, stepping out to the magnificent slope toward the Potomac, which forms his secluded back yard, knocks the golf balls around." A few years later, the *Washington Post* noted, "Mr. Harding golfed enough to do for several succeeding administrations. One winter, he played every course on the East Coast of Florida, from Jacksonville to Miami."

The Congress didn't complain, despite its history of preaching against the evils of golf. Instead, in the spring of 1922, the farmers were herded off the floors of both the Senate and the House so that their elected representatives could prepare for the official opening of the 406-acre Congressional Country Club, a private golf course in Maryland designed for the exclusive use of the members of Congress.

Not all Americans had their first taste of Daylight Saving at the insistence of the federal government. The earliest citywide experiments were conducted by Detroit and Cleveland in 1914, and throughout the United States, small towns, individual employers, merchant associations, and civic organizations altered their operating hours during the summer months as the allure of extended evenings spread. Nor were all Daylight pioneers residents of northeastern cities; municipal governments in Denver, Kansas City, and Chattanooga favored the idea. But isolation killed most of the early experiments. In the aftermath of the repeal of the wartime legislation, New York became the epicenter, and the slow conversion of cities occurred as an almost orderly southern and western progression, like sequentially illuminated dots on an otherwise dark map.

The rejection of Daylight Saving by rural and agricultural communities after the war was almost inevitable. It was not only that the promised fuel saving for homeowners had not materialized. Rural Americans were not connected to the electrical grid, and their homes were not outfitted with fuel lines. Unlike city dwellers, rural populations had not appreciably increased their consumption, so even if Daylight Saving saved fuel, it wouldn't have saved them much. And for farmworkers, more time in the sun was coals to Newcastle.

The invention of electrical generators and transformers in the nineteenth century heralded the advent of reliable artificial illumination, but it was not until 1935 that the technology was sufficiently affordable for the nation to undertake a program of rural electrification. And illuminating indoor spaces was one thing, but even in cities it proved much harder to defeat darkness outdoors. Many homes and most commercial buildings and major streets in urban America were fairly well lit by 1920, but parks, playgrounds, and many suburbs were dark. And many of mankind's favorite pastimes were not easily accommodated by indoor spaces—horse racing, for instance, and pole vaulting, not to mention baseball.

The opportunity to delay the start of major league baseball games by an hour—Daylight season has always tallied perfectly with the baseball season—promised increased attendance among school-age

fans and working adults. Instead of hastening the nationwide adoption of the clock change, however, the major leagues' immediate and
enduring affinity for Daylight Saving actually reinforced the distinction between cities in the Northeast and the rest of America. By 1920,
baseball was established as the National pastime. And you could play
baseball in Montana as well as in Massachusetts. But you couldn't
field a major league team in Billings or in any city further south or
west of Boston than the Red Sox could easily travel to by train. Even
as late as 1930, of the sixteen National League and American League
baseball teams, all were hosted by Daylight Saving cities in northern
states, with the exception of St. Louis and Washington, D.C.

During the first two seasons with Daylight Saving, the number of
tie games—an outcome despised by players and fans alike—dropped
from twenty-two to five in the major leagues, according to baseball
historian Clifford Blau. The extra hour translated into extra innings.
In succeeding seasons, less than 1 percent of all major league games
ended in ties. By every practical measure—attendance at major
league games, practice and play time for youth and school leagues,
enthusiasm of players for delayed starting times—Daylight Saving
was good for baseball. And baseball was good for Daylight Saving.
More than any single sport or hobby, baseball created a public, communal, almost daily habit of spending an extra hour in the sun.

The benefits to baseball persisted even after the first lights went
up in major league parks in 1935. Although it might seem sentimen-
tal or quaint to someone who first encountered the home team
under a retractable dome, major league owners, players, and fans
remained ambivalent about artificial illumination for many years,
and that extra hour of afternoon daylight was time enough to preserve the old ideal of the golden boys of summer. Until 1950, "the
number of night games was small and lights were not allowed to be
used to complete day or twilight games," explained Clifford Blau. "It
is hard to comprehend from our perspective that in the 1930's and
1940's, during twi-night doubleheaders, sometimes the first game

was called for darkness and minutes later the lights were switched on so the second game could be played."

The residents of 1600 Pennsylvania Avenue were all savvy enough to see to it that they were seen as baseball fans. But after Woodrow Wilson lost the battle for national Daylight Saving in 1919, the American League's Washington Senators were deprived of those precious extra afternoon innings. For the next ten years, Washington, D.C., often debated but never adopted Daylight Saving.

Warren G. Harding was frequently spotted in the stands during the Senators' games, and he entertained Babe Ruth at the White House on many occasions. Despite his love of baseball and golf, the president turned a deaf ear to the annual pleas for Daylight in the District of Columbia. This might seem hypocritical. After all, most residents of Washington who shared his passion for sport worked longer hours than the president did, and they would have benefited from an extra dose of late-day daylight. But no one ever accused Warren G. Harding of hypocrisy. He never hid his peccadilloes; he never even bothered to hide his Scotch. Despite Prohibition, President Harding typically poured himself a drink or three while playing a round of golf. He famously drank enough during at least one of his twice-weekly card games in the White House with his "Poker Cabinet" to lose a set of china acquired by Benjamin Harrison.

A few years before his public indiscretions boiled up into the Teapot Dome Scandal, Harding attempted to effect a compromise with the fans of Daylight Saving. He mandated voluntary Daylight Saving in the nation's capital, a laissez-faire approach that had often been recommended—facetiously—by opponents of the federal legislation. You could say it was a noble experiment, or you could say it was a Republican's idea of the perfect government program, as it only nominally involved the government and it didn't involve any programming.

The response from the *Woman Citizen* in May 1922 was not enthusiastic.

> What this old city is puzzling its head about is whether or not the President is going to disappear from his private golf practice an hour earlier, dine earlier, and go to bed an hour ahead of time, now that this queer daylight saving has been decreed by Presidential order for the District of Columbia. No clocks are to be set ahead, and no official order changed, but the good faith of the community is called upon to look at the clock and call it an hour earlier; report at work an hour earlier, go home and go to bed on faith—in order to avoid calling the plan "Daylight Saving," which the farmers abhor and which raises such a rumpus in Congress.

Many residents of Washington, D.C., were confounded. In defense of its hometown and its leading citizen, the *Washington Post* initially adopted a slightly pontifical tone toward New York and the other renegade cities that had embraced postwar Daylight Saving and divided the nation. "Irrespective of the arguments pro and con in the matter of daylight saving, there can be no question of the fact that it is conducive to immense confusion, annoyance, and in many instances to serious embarrassment on the fifty-fifty plan," the editors began on 7 May 1922. "Cities and states could, of course, effect the same saving of daylight by simply keeping the clock on sun time and starting the day's work an hour earlier than customary.... In the interest of less confusion and the combating of general cussedness, this is what should be done."

For the next few weeks, the *Post* chronicled the strange saga. The banks were among the first institutions to announce new, earlier opening and closing hours; the public utilities soon revised their schedules; the district and municipal courts fell into line, though there was no general agreement among federal magistrates. Most retail stores opted for the new schedule, but grocery stores opted out. The public school schedule did not change, and the hours of operation at most government departments and executive offices were set back by an hour, though the printing office led a small band of federal-government refuseniks. No clocks were altered. People were expected to get up one hour earlier than normal. However, passenger train schedules were altered. Streetcar schedules were not, so operators were on their own; they had to guess when most commuters would be waiting at which stop for a ride. The cinemas and theaters announced that there would be no change in show times. Caught between their colleagues in the American League and their namesakes in anti-Daylight Congress, the Washington Senators decided to start their home baseball games half an hour earlier than normal.

Then, on the very day before the plan was to take effect, the banks decided not to open early. Two days later, several district courts abandoned their newly adopted opening and closing times. The streetcar operators had to guess again. It became impossible for anyone to predict at what time any office or store might open or close. For almost two months the mayhem continued, with a marked decline daily in participation in the plan. When the Federal Employees Union finally turned to the White House for advice, President Harding announced that department heads throughout the government should feel free to set their opening and closing times without seeking his approval. After that, the District resisted the charms of Daylight Saving for several decades.

When he proposed his daylight-saving plan for Paris in 1784, Ben Franklin predicted that "all the difficulty will be in the first two or three days." But by 1930, the nation's capital was badly out of sync with other northeastern cities, which were running an hour ahead of the rest of the nation for five months a year. The Congress refused to act as an intermediary. Perhaps it was as confused as the rest of the country; everything it had attempted to do about time had produced an inverse effect. It renounced Daylight Saving, and immediately thereafter, no city that adopted the clock change ever gave the habit up. It denounced golf, which corresponded precisely with the onset of a decade-long, nationwide golf craze—well, everywhere but Pennsylvania Avenue. As the *Washington Post* glumly noted in the spring of 1930, "golf has lost prestige in the White House since Warren G. Harding sheathed his blades for the last time, for Calvin Coolidge never had a club in his hands and Herbert Hoover's only known athletic indulgence is hurling the medicine ball against the abdomens of his Cabinet members."

"We suffer most," wrote H. L. Mencken, "when the White House busts with ideas."

In an attempt to promote physical fitness, Herbert Hoover eschewed every known sport and every recreational activity invented over the millennia, and he ignored the recreational potential of national Daylight Saving. Americans had demonstrated their eagerness to play baseball, golf, football, and tennis in the afternoon and evening. But instead of capitalizing on these healthy habits, every morning at seven o'clock, Hoover organized a half-hour session at an eight-foot-high net, where he and a few loyal members of his administration tossed and bounced and belted a six-pound medicine ball at each other. This ritual was billed by the president and his personal physician as an invigorating hybrid of volleyball, tennis, and ball-in-the-ring, a variation on "keep away" Hoover had seen played with medicine balls by sailors cooped up on navy ships. Hoover-ball was a symbolic sport, and it lasted about as long as Woodrow Wilson's flock of sheep.

"This is a poor taste in sport," complained the *Washington Post.*

Homer Green, a farmer who frequently submitted his "hollers" to the *New York Times,* saw no medicine balls in Middletown, New

York. But Homer and his fellow farmers did get "unmercifully het up at about 4 o'clock, God's time, but 5 o'clock golf time, when we see ... the many Government, State, county, and township employee contingents gleefully and swiftly sail by in their limousines, knowing we still have two more hours to struggle."

Turnabout is fair play. Much of the country would come to blame the farmers for Daylight Saving, and the farmers took to blaming the government. Fore!

When the Depression hit, the farm population began its endless decline; only one in five American workers was involved in agriculture, and in 1932, the most productive farmland in the country dried into a Dust Bowl. By the end of the century, there would be fewer than 5 million farmers in America—about 2 percent of the labor force—and almost 30 million golfers. In 2000, the value of agricultural goods produced by the average farm was hovering near $100,000; the average golf course was bringing in $1 million a year. And the number of Americans living on farms was approximately equal to the number of Americans who were permanent residents of golf-course communities.

Chapter Six

Mean Time

Nothing puzzles me more than time and space; and yet nothing puzzles me less, for I never think about them.

—CHARLES LAMB, 1810

When you think about it, there's something wrong with time. You don't have to be a physicist to spot the oddities. Look at a calendar: September, October, November, December. The names of these months come to us directly from the Latin. But we have a correspondence problem. Our ninth month is named for seven (*septem*), the tenth for eight (*octo*), the eleventh for nine (*novem*), and the twelfth for ten (*decem*). The Roman calendar was a famously inaccurate stew of religious and political ambitions, with only 304 days, ten months, and an unspecified catchall period at the end of this so-called year. These extra days were eventually codified into January and February, originally as the eleventh and twelfth months. But the duration of these two months was constantly altered to lengthen or abbreviate the terms of political appointees, and after many years of manipulation, January had migrated into the autumn. The Romans ultimately developed a 365-day calendar, borrowing from the Egyptians, who had managed this feat about five thousand years earlier. Like most calendars, the revised Roman-Julian version relied on the occasional insertion of a longer year, a leap year. Even with these adjustments, though, it was not until the sixteenth century that the Roman kinks were worked out, largely thanks to Pope Gregory, who had the leap years recalibrated and, to set things aright, waved his holy hand and eliminated 10 days from the year 1582. Unlike Daylight Saving, this new Gregorian calendar was not an immediate hit in Great Britain, where papal powers were suspect. Calendars in England and the colonies remained 11 days out of sync with those of other nations until 1752.

What is a month? Again, look at a calendar. One month appears to be an annually recurring sequence of days ranging in number from 28 to 31. Months were originally based on lunar cycles. The Maori worked with a strictly lunar calendar, but because there are roughly 12 1/2 lunar cycles in any given year, their New Year's Day changed annually, and they occasionally needed a thirteenth month. Contemporary lunar calendars are principally used to maintain religious and ceremonial traditions. Like the Egyptians, the ancient Chinese and the Maya used solar and astronomical observations to produce 365-day calendars that were not marred by irregular lunar months. Instead their calendars used recurring periods of 60 or 20 days, rounded off by predictable leap days as needed.

What is a month? It depends on how you look at it. A lunar month is the average time between two full moons, or approximately 29 days, 12 hours, and 44 minutes. A solar month is the time lapse between two passages of the sun through the vernal equinox, or about 30 days, 10 hours, 29 minutes, and 3.8 seconds. A sidereal (star-based) month is the time it takes for the moon to complete one revolution around the earth as measured by the observation of a fixed star, which adds up to something like 27 days, 7 hours, and 43 minutes.

These profound variations and complications have been with us for centuries, and yet in the twentieth century, the most sustained public controversy about time focused on one allegedly saved hour of daylight. The moderns were not unaware of their ancestors. "If Congress turned as often to Roman precedent as did the fathers of the republic," editorialized *The Nation* in 1918, "the Daylight-Saving bill would have passed long ago; for the Romans were confirmed daylight-savers." Like many cultures, the Romans divided daylight into twelve equal hours, so that each hour varied seasonally from 45 to 75 minutes, lengthening as the earth tilted Rome toward summer. And "Roman occupations of the day being arranged with reference to sunrise," continued *The Nation*:

> The Roman who began work with the fourth hour, would on the longest day of the year, when the sun rose at about 4:50 A.M. and set at 7:50 P.M., reach his *officina* at 8:35; on the shortest day, when it rose at 7:40 A.M. and set about 5 P.M., he would be there about 9:50. Thus was accomplished in summer a saving of an hour and a quarter.

Daylight Saving also prompted scores of world travelers and amateur horologists to write to their hometown newspapers and describe the adaptable water clocks of ancient China and the Japanese pillar clocks with movable hour markers, which were adjusted almost daily so that the sun rose at 6 A.M. every day of the year. "In other clocks imported from the West," one correspondent reported to the *New York Times*, "they changed the speed of the clock every few weeks, so that as the sun got into his early rising habits the clock hand followed and thereby assisted in the operation of forcing lazy members of Far Eastern families out of their beds that they might do their proper share of the world's work."

As early as 3000 B.C.E., the Sumerians had divided the day into twelve two-hour periods, but other cultures lavished most of their timekeeping attention on daylight hours, which were often keyed to periods of prayer. The twenty-four-hour day was not widely observed until 1600. And just about one hundred years later, pendulum clocks of unprecedented reliability were produced, and their owners noticed that something was wrong with most twenty-four-hour days—they weren't twenty-four hours long.

We are accustomed to the charming idea that a day is the time it takes our spinning planet to complete one revolution on its imaginary axis. But if you keep your eye on a fixed star, you will see that the earth completes its rotation in twenty-three hours and fifty-six minutes—a sidereal day. If you mark your position on the earth and wait for the sun to reappear at that point, you'll have to wait for the earth to perform one complete revolution—a sidereal day—and a little more, because our planet is orbiting the sun, and it takes anywhere from three to four additional minutes of rotation time to bring your designated spot back into alignment with the sun. This is one solar day. It is never precisely three or four minutes longer than a sidereal day, because the earth is tilted, its orbit around the sun is elliptical, and the earth's orbital speed is variable. In all ways, the earth is an irregular orb. Averaged out over the course of a year, though, its irregularities produce a mean solar day of almost exactly twenty-four hours.

Mechanical clock time never really was sun time. Clock time is mean time. Thus, depending on your specific location on the earth, over the course of a year, a clock will differ substantially from a sundial, sometimes by more than fifteen minutes. Sundials show you your place in the sun. Clocks make every day an average day.

We often want to know what time it is, though most of us don't know what time is. It's not that we don't value our time. Time is a precious currency, and we entrust it to the experts. Astronomers and physicists are our temporal stockbrokers. Time is out of our hands— or most of it is. The principal reason Daylight Saving has created such enduring and impassioned confusion is that we are compelled to meddle with our clocks, to take time into our hands twice a year and, inevitably, to wonder about the fate of that hour.

"It sounds boastful, but the physicist has sort of cleared up the things that take about an hour," Williams College physics professor David Park told the *Washington Post* in April 1985, on the eve of the annual clock change. "The cutting edge of physics deals with time that is inconceivably short or long—timing elementary particles or the whole cosmos. The hour falls right in between."

It falls to us.

For the experts, the hour is a unit of measurement, a convenient way to express the sum of 3,600 atomically calculated seconds, or 1/24 of an exquisitely calibrated day. It has no independent meaning. An hour cannot be accurately defined without reference to smaller or larger units of measurement.

But for practical purposes, the hour has been objectified. It is no longer just a unit of measure; in our hands, it has become a standard of measurement, and blunt as it is, we use the hour to evaluate almost every feature of our daily lives. For the last one hundred years, mathematicians and scientists have pursued time intervals of infinitesimally tiny and inconceivably vast proportions. A second—long understood as 1/86,400 of the mean solar day—has been redefined several times, but our standard hour has been unaffected. In the 1950s, reliable atomic timescales were produced, and that's when time really got away from us. After that, the sun no longer defined the second; the element cesium defined the second as the duration of 9,192,631,770 periods of the radiation corresponding to the transition between two hyperfine levels of the ground state of the cesium-133 atom.

The standards of most earthlings are somewhat less exacting. Since 1884, we've been living with standardized time, manufactured twenty-four-hour periods that are so mean—so average, and therefore unlike the irregular solar day—that they occasioned a day of two noons, and they regularly feature such incongruities as two entirely different dates for people separated by a few miles, and days that run on for more than fifty-five hours.

"The National Bureau of Standards knows very beautifully how long a second is," Professor David Park reassured the *Washington Post* in 1985. "But the Earth doesn't know it very well."

The modern project of standardization was well under way by the end of the eighteenth century. The surface of the earth, including the oceans, had been effectively mapped and measured by the intersecting lines of latitude and longitude, which normalized and expedited international trade and travel. In 1792, the French devised and adopted the metric system, which gradually became the worldwide standard for weights and measures, with a few nations standing as notable exceptions, including Great Britain and the United States. (The French also proposed a revolutionary calendar based on a year divided into ten-day weeks, thereby eliminating the Christian bias in the seven-day week of the Gregorian calendar, and thereby ensuring the new calendar's own demise, as most French people preferred to get a day of rest on every seventh rather than every tenth day.) In 1798, in his firearms factory in Connecticut, Eli Whitney pioneered the use of standardized, interchangeable parts, inventing a way of making things that foreshadowed the mass-production methods to come. The utility of practicable manufacturing standards informed the course of industrial development. The intercontinental railroad was a dramatic illustration of the need for reliable standards in every detail, from the gauge of the rails to the width of the tracks as they were laid by laborers separated by thousands of miles. This lesson was replayed as telegraph lines, electrical cables, and telephone wires were strung across the landscape during the second half of the nineteenth century. The commercial and social exploitation of travel, communication, and trade increasingly relied on the adoption of consistent methods and compatible materials. By the time genuinely national and international networks were formed, uniformity was not only economically advantageous; it was the surest way to promote safety and convenience.

A new, standardized day had dawned, though rarely at a predictable hour.

"I address you on a subject which causes some inconvenience here...the irregularity and diversity of time," wrote a correspondent to the *North American Review* in 1815:

> There is no common standard, and every district is regulated by a clock of its own. The difference between time in Boston and the villages about it is always considerable, and in some instances it varies upward of half an hour. There is this difference at least between Boston and Salem [15 miles to the north]; this often interferes with appointments in business, and in certain circumstances a criminal might be able to prove an alibi on this ground.

No president and no Congress attempted to heal these breaches, which were ever more apparent as technologies narrowed the communications gap between people. For most of the nineteenth century, the courts were left to decide which time was the legally binding time in criminal, contractual, and liability cases involving contradictory local interpretations of onsets, deadlines, and expiration dates. No consistent standard emerged.

Many nations established an official national time based on a line of longitude, or meridian, passing through or near the capital city, but local timekeepers often ignored these standards. Still, by 1850, Great Britain had largely succeeded in establishing Greenwich Mean Time for England, Scotland, and Wales—a uniform clock time based on the mean solar day at Britain's venerable Royal Observatory in Greenwich, a London suburb. Germany and other European nations were attempting to coordinate local, railroad, and national times, as well. Of course, a single national time could not reasonably be applied to countries spanning great east-west distances, like Russia, Canada, and the United States. And it was the railroads, whose passenger and freight lines inadvertently picked up and transported the local time of one city and then another and then another, that most desperately needed a regionally coordinated system of timekeeping. Scheduling was guesswork. They knew how long it would take a train to travel fifteen miles from Boston, but they had no way of predicting the local time at which that train would arrive in Salem or anywhere in between. By 1869, when the tracks of the Union and Pacific railroads converged, completing the transcontinental link, these little annoyances had assumed massive proportions.

Charles F. Dowd, principal of a seminary for girls in Saratoga, New York, is credited with the first proposal to divide the nation into regional time zones. But it was the Scottish-born Canadian Sandford Fleming who produced a detailed, worldwide system based on twenty-four meridians, each one hour apart. Fleming was a genuine polymath—statesman, railroad man, civil engineer, and visionary. Integral to his remarkable plan, which he first worked out in 1876 and continued to refine for years, was the adoption of a twenty-four-hour clock that would keep "Uniform Non-Local (Terrestrial) Time."

However, the time-zone plan that was adopted for North America on 11 October 1883 by the General Time Convention, a forerunner of the American Railway Association, was proposed by its chairman, W. F. Allen. This version was custom-tailored to the scheduling, switching, and safety concerns of the North American railroads. Most important, Allen's proposed time zones tallied with the regional divisions of the separately owned and operated railroad lines. Allen also foresaw the need for elastic boundaries between the four zones in the United States—adjustable at the discretion of the railroads—and he retained the popular twelve-hour method of time-keeping. Each new time zone was roughly fifteen degrees of latitude wide, measured from a designated midpoint, a meridian that established the average noon—mean solar time—for the territory included in the zone.

The plan was not subject to the approval of the national or state legislatures. No popular referendum was held. This proposal not only promised to reduce America's many local times into four standard times; in effect, it consolidated the United States into four distinct economic regions. Considering the response of farmers, laborers, homemakers, and their elected representatives thirty-five years later, when the comparatively minor Daylight Saving reform was proposed, it is surprising that the mere proposal to eliminate local time and replace it with zoned time did not incite rioting in the streets. But on Sunday, 18 November 1883, one month after the railroad convention approved the plan, clocks in the most easterly cities of the United States marked noon on local time as they always had, and as the sun passed over the 75th meridian (which runs quite nearly through Philadelphia), those clocks were set back from their various local times to their second noon of the day, the new mean time, the shared standard noon. Clocks in the western half of the Eastern Time Zone were advanced to that same new noon, regardless of the sun's position in the sky.

A telegraphic flash was emitted from the Naval Observatory in Washington, D.C., coordinating Eastern noon with 11:00 A.M. Central, 10:00 Mountain, and 9:00 Pacific time in zones bisected by the 90th, 105th, and 120th meridians. "It was a bold stroke," crowed the *Indianapolis Sentinel:*

> To regulate the time of this Empire Republic of the World is an undertaking of magnificent proportions. Railroad time is to be the time of the future. The Sun is no longer to boss the job. People— 55,000,000 of them—must eat, sleep, and work as well as travel by

railroad time. It is a revolt, a rebellion. The sun will be requested to rise and set by railroad time. The planets must, in the future, make their circuits by such timetables as railroad magnates arrange.

Maybe this was the apotheosis of Manifest Destiny in the popular imagination. The locomotive had been the engine of the continental conquest. And within a generation, this unorthodox, unscientific, and unearthly idea of an hour perpetrated by the railroads for their own benefit would be enshrined as real time, sun time, God's time. Seventy of the one hundred principal cities in the United States adopted their new time-zone times immediately, according to *Scientific American,* and eighty of those cities were in sync within five months. There were doomsayers and naysayers. Some of the opposition came from Christian preachers, most of it was local and fleeting, and none of it was effectively organized.

"It is a preconceived idea with many that there is a simultaneous Sunday over the earth, and that Christians in every meridian keep the Lord's day at one and the same time," wrote Sandford Fleming in the *Smithsonian Report* in 1886. "Facts, however, establish this as a mistake."

As Fleming wrote about the troubles to come in "Time-Reckoning in the Twentieth Century," most of his contemporaries believed that the worldwide time confusion had just recently been sorted out and solved, and most of them credited Sandford Fleming with the solution. Two years earlier, in October 1884, at a Washington, D.C., conference attended by representatives of twenty-five nations, Fleming's impeccable proposal for a single, worldwide "cosmopolitan time" had been taken up for the umpteenth time by geographers, astronomers, railroaders, and government officials. The conferees were impressed by the example of the railroads in North America, and though they had no power to enforce their recommendations, they endorsed a zonal system based on several points from Fleming's proposal. Before the end of the decade, their standardized time zones were dictating local time in almost every nation in the world.

As Fleming had imagined it could be, the surface of the earth was divided into twenty-four time zones corresponding to the twenty-four hours of the mean solar day. Because the obliging earth was a sphere, its 360-degree circumference yielded twenty-four equal segments, each approximately 15 degrees wide. Each zone was defined not by its eastern or western boundary but by its center, an imaginary line, or meridian, that ran from the North Pole to the South Pole. As in the American model, the eastern and western boundaries were flexible; each zone's central meridian—from which noon was measured—was fixed.

To begin, one line of longitude was drawn from the North Pole to the South Pole; this was the zero-degree meridian. From zero, they measured out 7 1/2 degrees east and 7 1/2 degrees west, and that defined the first 15-degree time zone. When the sun reached its apex at the zero meridian (more precisely, at mean solar noon at that line), all clocks in that zone would show the time as noon. Next, meridians were drawn 15 degrees east and west of zero, and two new zones were created, each extending 7 1/2 degrees east and west from their meridians. When it was noon at zero degrees, it was 1:00 P.M. in the abutting zone to the east and 11:00 A.M. in the abutting zone to the west. Counting off the meridians east and west from zero to 180 was a small but significant adaptation; if the zones had been created by moving around the globe in one direction, zero would also have been the 360-degree meridian, and as Fleming pointed out, there was already plenty of confusion embedded in this allegedly simplified version of his scheme.

The most obvious complication for the men who drew the lines on the globe and divided the earth into zones was history. Many artists had preceded them. The globe had already been divided many times into political entities—empires, nations, states, and cities, whose boundaries were as irregular and unreliable as the men who ruled or wanted to rule these entities. And the 1884 conferees could only suggest a zone or zones for independent nations; it was up to each one to decide for itself whether it would accept its designated mean time. What's more, there were practical considerations. In 1883, the American railroaders had attempted to create zones in which major cities were near the meridians, with the less populated, rural land occupying the farther-out eastern and western areas. Although Congress would later be blamed for it, by 1883 the discrepancy between clock time and sun time was already more profound for farmers than for urbanites. But the American plan did not suit all city dwellers, either; residents of Detroit so resented their placement outside Eastern Time that the city refused to adopt its designated Central Time until 1905—and the city never permanently settled in to this zone.

The original worldwide time zones represented an attempt to respect national boundaries and avoid splitting nations into multiple zones where possible. And everyone recognized that time coordination also had commercial implications for bordering nations. To this day, the boundaries are elastic in the extreme; they zig and zag dramatically, and at some points, the boundary of one zone nearly meets the central meridian of a neighboring zone. It is almost impossible to keep track of these imaginary lines, as nations can simply alter their clock time as they see fit—another bend in a boundary line. But because the meridians never move, the system's stability is preserved; a single change by a nation or city does not alter the mean (meridian) time for anyone else in the zone.

Still, from the start, it was evident that zone times not only differed dramatically from local sun times, but were also egregiously bad approximations of the new mean times that the zones were meant to impose. This is still obvious today in the first three zones—based on the zero meridian, and the meridians 15 degrees east and west—which include most of the countries represented at the 1884 conference.

England falls entirely within the boundaries of the zero-degree zone. Iceland is west of the boundary for this zone; when it is noon in England, according to zone time, it should be 10:00 and 11:00 A.M. on Iceland's western and eastern coasts. Instead, Iceland has been shoved into England's zone, so it is noon all over Iceland, as it is in many countries that lie west of England—and west of the original western boundary of the zero zone. When it should be 11:00 A.M., the clocks read noon in Ireland, Portugal, Liberia, Sierra Leone, Guinea, Guinea Bissau, Gambia, Senegal, Western Sahara, and a number of other nations. Thus, many countries inadvertently practiced year-round Daylight Saving as early as 1884, decades before it was invented. Similarly, Spain, Belgium, Luxembourg, the Netherlands, France, Benin, and Monaco all lie within the boundaries of the zone occupied by England, but have been assigned to the neighboring zone, 15 degrees west, an effort to secure a single time zone for most of the continental Western European nations. When it is noon in England, it should be noon in these and many similarly situated nations to their north and south; however, in their adopted zone it is 1:00 P.M.— another batch of year-round daylight savers. And most of these nations turn their clocks ahead with the rest of us each spring, doubling their advantage.

And these are just a few of the peculiarities in just three of the twenty-four time zones.

The principal controversy in 1884 was supposed to involve a debate about where in the world each day began. Where was ground zero? Navigators and mapmakers over the centuries had used different points of origin—established by the prime meridian, or zero line of longitude—in their renderings of the globe. The prime meridian turned up in Rhodes, the Canary Islands, and cities from St. Petersburg to Philadelphia. The location of the prime meridian did not affect the accuracy or utility of a map; it was largely a choice of convenience (near the home of the mapmaker or sailor) or an honorific designation (to please the sponsoring empire, for instance).

Despite the plethora of established prime meridians, there were only three serious candidates in 1884. One suggestion was to place the prime meridian in neutral territory, somewhere in the Pacific Ocean. France suggested the Paris meridian, which was used by nearly 10 percent of the commercial freighters in the world. Greenwich, England, however, was the prime meridian of choice for almost 75 percent of the world's sea trade. Twenty-two of the twenty-five votes at the 1884 conference approved the choice of Greenwich. This established Greenwich Mean Time (GMT) as the zero hour for the rest of the world. Clock time in all other nations has since been reported as GMT plus or minus some number of hours. France did not vote against its competitor. Along with Brazil, France abstained when the vote was taken, so no one could accuse the French of being bad sports, though they did not adopt the Greenwich meridian for several decades. And in that final vote in 1884, the French colony of Saint-Domingue (later, Haiti) cast a single vote against Greenwich. This dissenting vote had no practical effect, but it did mean France didn't have to suffer British boasts about a unanimous victory.

The establishment of the prime meridian also established, by default, the 180-degree meridian as the international date line. The date in the Eastern Hemisphere, to the left of this imaginary line, is one day ahead of the date in the Western Hemisphere. This strange feature of timekeeping has often been exploited in fiction, most famously by Jules Verne; it determines the result of the contest to travel *Around the World in Eighty Days*. Of course, the date line itself is a fiction. It asserts that the residents of islands and atolls separated by only a few miles are experiencing two entirely different days of the week.

Since at least the fourteenth century, sailors were befuddled by the phenomenon that became known as the circumnavigator's paradox. The date books of those who sailed westward around the world, when compared with the calendars at home, were missing one day; one more day had passed than was recorded in their logs. In effect, sailing west, the voyagers had lost a day. Sailors who traveled eastward around the world inevitably gained a day; that is, if they arrived home on Tuesday according to their logs, they discovered it was Monday.

Time zones did not create the need for the absurd convention of a date line, and the people who brought us time zones could have eliminated it. It is not used or observed by military timekeepers, scientists, national governments, or any international business that has adopted a version of Universal Time—the modern name for the "cosmopolitan time" proposed by Sandford Fleming. His proposal for Universal Time required the adoption of a twenty-four-hour clock, which he considered just one of its advantages. "The halving of the day has doubtless been long in use," he wrote in 1886, "but beyond its claim to antiquity, it is a custom that confers not a single benefit."

Universal Time acknowledges the commonsense notion that a single, complete revolution of the earth on its axis is what we mean by a day. And a day is a discrete item; we can have only one at a time. According to Universal Time, when it is 10:00 in London, it is 10:00 in Beijing, and 10:00 in New York. Using Universal Time, everyone on the earth is living in the same moment on the same date—which really is the truth of our situation. With Greenwich as our prime meridian, this means at 10:00 Universal Time it is midmorning in London (10:00 A.M. local time), the middle of the night in Beijing (11:00 P.M. local time), and dawn in New York (5:00 A.M. local time).

The experts thought the rest of us would not be able to handle this. And yet a similar discrepancy inheres in our universal names for the months. December designates the twelfth month of the year in both America and Australia, but we don't expect a December day in Detroit to resemble a December day Down Under. The quantity and quality of daylight in December vary according to your location on the earth. By the end of the nineteenth century, almost all nations had adopted the universal twelve-month calendar. Sandford Fleming figured they would be able to handle a universal twenty-four-hour day.

Fleming suggested the use of the letters of the alphabet (skipping *I* and *V*) instead of numbers to designate the twenty-four hours, to help wean people from their association of a particular hour with a particular amount of sunlight. He and later advocates of Universal Time also proposed the selection of a more neutral prime meridian (such as the current date line) so that all nations, including Great Britain, would have to endure a similar period of adjustment to the twenty-four-hour day. Universal Time proponents have also suggested the use of two-faced watches or double-dial clocks designed to display both Universal Time and local time.

The experts took to Universal Time; today, it is one of many refined and customized timekeeping systems, whose names run the alphabet, from atomic time to Zulu time. The rest of us were given civil time—which is mean time, which is a bunch of standardized hours. As a bonus, we got that infernal date line. And if you think about it, as Sandford Fleming did, all of this doesn't add up to a single day:

> Sunday has been discovered to run over some fifty-five hours. The same may be said of any day of the week; and as a consequence we have, taking the whole globe into view, Saturday and Monday running over into the intervening Sunday to overlap each other about seven hours. We have, in fact as a constant occurrence, portions of three consecutive days co-existent. . . . [As the London *Times* reported] A telegraph message dated Simla, 1:55 A.M. Wednesday, was received in London at 11:47 P.M. on Tuesday. As the clerk said, with pardonable confusion, "Why, this message was sent off to-morrow."

Chapter Seven

Split Decisions

Time makes more converts than reason.
—THOMAS PAINE, 1776

$\mathcal{I}$n the aftermath of the stock market crash, a few enterprising young men in North Carolina applied to the Chamber of Commerce for the right to form a youth chapter in Raleigh. As soon as the junior chamber received a charter, those young entrepreneurs launched a quest for the Holy Grail of retail, venturing into territory where their elders had suffered numerous defeats. They organized a petition drive on behalf of Daylight Saving. Their signature campaign was so successful that the city commissioners reversed their long-standing opposition to Daylight and ordered everyone in Raleigh to spring forward in early May 1932.

Not everyone in Raleigh had signed that petition, and a few of the disgruntled dissenters requested a meeting with town officials. "Opponents did not bother with petitions," reported the *New York Times,* "but descended upon the city in numbers sufficient to overflow the building and to cause the Commissioners to end the hearing abruptly with the statement that they had heard enough." Four days after its inauguration, Daylight Saving was abandoned in Raleigh and, effectively, in all of North Carolina, as the majority in the state legislature was held by representatives of rural districts. Tennessee, Alabama, and a few other southern states temporarily adopted Daylight Saving as an emergency economic measure at the request of the White House, but the region was resistant to its permanent appeal. Georgia refused to adopt even temporary Daylight Saving, even as an emergency measure, even after a personal request from President Roosevelt.

The dawn of Daylight Saving had stalled in America. Cities with long traditions of almost adopting the clock change—from Baltimore to Denver—continued to debate and to demur throughout the 1930s. By the spring of 1937, residents in at least some parts of eighteen states turned their clocks ahead, and the total number of participating cities in many of these states had more than doubled. But the gains were typically realized in northeastern metropolitan areas with long-established preferences for extended evenings. Experiments with Daylight Saving in other regions of the country were few and reliably short-lived.

Proponents of Daylight looked west for hope, to the fast-growing cities of California. The movie industry in Los Angeles remained vehemently opposed. In 1930, in a letter to the *San Francisco Examiner,* Fox–West Coast president Harold Franklin had protested the newspaper's editorial endorsement of Daylight Saving. He estimated that it "cuts theatre receipts from ten to thirty percent right off the gross," and warned it "has unlimited possibilities for evil to us." Franklin had a penchant for overstatement. By the late 1930s, he was at Columbia Pictures, where he was responsible for producing an industrywide promotional campaign; every year it was titled *Motion Pictures' Greatest Year.* But by 1940, California's vast economy was diverse, and the state had already begun to experience the water and electricity shortfalls that would plague it through the end of the century and beyond. When a statewide referendum on Daylight was called for November 1940, many political observers believed it would not only pass but provoke a coast-to-coast conversion.

It wasn't even close. Californians voted down Daylight by a two-to-one margin. That year, the total number of states with some form of Daylight Saving fell to fifteen. It would take another world war to persuade most Americans to submit to the clock change. And yet for millions of Americans who had rejected Daylight Saving, and above millions of acres of pasture and farmland, the sun rose and set an hour later than God had intended.

When Congress passed the 1918 law "To Save Daylight and to Provide Standard Time for the United States," the legislators charged the Interstate Commerce Commission (ICC) with the task of calibrating and recalibrating the time zones to suit the needs of business in general, and to respond to the particular concerns of the railroads. National Daylight Saving was repealed in 1919, but the Standard Time legislation remained in effect. Not only was the ICC instructed to standardize the time zones that had evolved at the discretion of the railroads since 1883, but it was specifically instructed to arbitrate proposed changes to the boundaries according to "the convenience of commerce."

In its initial go at this, the ICC moved all the time-zone boundaries west in 1919. As a result, the clocks of everyone who lived in the eastern reaches of the Central, Mountain, and Pacific zones were advanced by one hour—and they were never pushed back. This created a permanent, year-round form of Daylight Saving for citizens of the Central, Mountain, and Pacific Time zones—regions of the country that had repeatedly expressed their moral and economic objections to the clock change.

This phenomenon did not figure in the ongoing debate about Daylight Saving. The uproar occasioned by the passage and repeal of the national Daylight legislation had diverted attention away from the work of the ICC. For almost fifty years, the ICC orchestrated the manipulation of the Standard Time zones in relative obscurity.

One of the ICC's goals in 1919 had been to establish the boundaries in undeveloped areas, where commerce would not be complicated by conflicting clock times. Over the years, however, population growth and economic development inevitably eroded the commission's success and necessitated additional changes. These changes typically led to more people advancing their clocks. And right from the start, there were hundreds of small towns on the newly designated borders, and an assignment to one time zone or the other often seemed to residents more of a coin toss than a considered decision.

The ICC was not just splitting hairs. It stretched the western boundary of the Eastern Time Zone almost to the breaking point to include Michigan and much of Ohio. As a result, the former Central Time residents in these states experienced noon at the same moment that people in Bangor and Miami did. Detroit became an Eastern Time city. This newly drawn boundary between the Eastern and Central zones also chopped entire states in half, from Indiana to Florida.

A few years later, Cincinnati felt a little forlorn, and the time gap between it and Cleveland, which was operating on Eastern Time, was judged a commercial inconvenience, so Cincinnati was designated as an Eastern city. It was no surprise that by the spring of 1932, Chicago traders were grumbling about the bad luck of being an hour behind New York and other eastern cities as they tried to work their way out of the Depression.

But in that spring of 1932, Mrs. Anna Larson was the timely story in Chicago. On 24 April, while climbing a ladder to change her clock, she broke a rung and broke her neck. On the same day, according to his friends, William Stultz also died of Daylight Saving. He'd spent the day in Marietta, Pennsylvania, collecting more than two hundred signatures for a petition drive to repeal Daylight Saving, went to his club to meet with other Daylight opponents, and died of a heart attack.

These and lesser inconveniences and oddities credited to Daylight Saving were reported every spring and fall, and they were irksome and entertaining enough to keep the Daylight debate alive during the 1930s. The New York State Supreme Court set aside a foreclosure because the debtor had been served with papers on a train after 11:00 P.M. on Saturday. The train was operating on Eastern Standard Time. But in the debtor's hometown, thanks to Daylight Saving, it was after midnight and, therefore, it was Sunday, and papers could not be served on a Sunday. Bars and nightclubs argued (usually unsuccessfully) that their closing times should be an hour later in the summer, as the licensing laws that forced them to shut down at 2:00 or 3:00 A.M. specified Standard Time. In Rochester, a Buffalo resident parked his car in a space clearly posted as legal after 9:30 A.M. He checked his watch. It was 10:20 A.M. When he later appeared before a judge, the *New York Times* reported, "he said he did not know whether to plead guilty or not guilty; he might be wrong in Rochester, but he would be right in Buffalo. Judge Tompkins reminded him he was in Rochester," but he suspended the penalty.

These anecdotes were much more memorable than reports from Washington, D.C., about the latest longitudinal determination from the ICC. And the peculiarities of Daylight Saving cropped up twice a year in hundreds of cities. The alteration of a time zone affected only a particular locality, and just once. So the country continued to blame Daylight Saving for its time troubles as, almost unnoticed, the time zone boundaries continued to move west, advancing the hands of all clocks in their path.

By February 1936, the business community in Chicago was fed up with the city's inconvenient location in the Central Time Zone. At the urging of Chicago businesses, a petition for the inclusion of Chicago in the Eastern Time Zone was submitted to the ICC. Impatient for the commission's decision, the Chicago City Council passed a local ordinance ordering residents to advance their clocks on the first day of March. Although no one in Chicago had the legal authority to change the time zone, the city could prescribe year-round Daylight Saving, and the effect was the same. Instead of shifting ahead for only five months, Chicagoans shifted ahead for the entire year.

That year, the sun allegedly rose and set in Chicago and Cape Cod at the same moment. The railroads serving metropolitan Chicago refused to accept this proposition, but most suburban communities did adopt the new, unofficial Eastern Standard Time. And then April arrived, and the Chicago Stock Exchange and the Board of Trade defied the rest of the city and immoderately sprang ahead again, to keep up with Daylight Saving Time in New York. The clocks of those traders and brokers on the banks of Lake Michigan were then one hour ahead of clocks in Miami; Atlanta; Washington, D.C.; and all the Atlantic Coast communities that did not observe Daylight Saving.

In August, the ICC refused to stretch Eastern Standard Time that far. "Chicago is so definitely inside the Central time zone that there is no valid reason for authorizing a shift," editorialized the *Washington Post,* sounding a little defensive about its relatively slow clocks. "The effect of [Chicago's] daylight-saving ordinance upon local train schedules and upon the commercial activities of nearby farm areas is confusing enough." In November 1936, Chicago put the question to voters, who asked to be returned to Central Time. In 1937, the city passed a relatively modest Daylight Saving ordinance for the summer months.

That same spring, the Daylight issue again seized the District of Columbia and a number of nearby cities. The *Washington Post* ran a feature story on the controversy. It began with some suggested topics for starting an argument, ranging from the Pulitzer Prize to children's IQ scores:

Yet, in all fairness to, and with full acknowledgement of the indisputable merits of the aforementioned subjects as scrap-kindlers, it is respectfully submitted herewith that the surest way to start a battle in Washington today is to stand up and say: I am in favor of daylight saving time in the District of Columbia. . . . [T]he present stew finds mother arrayed against daughter, father against son, an internecine squabble that waxes more ferocious daily in the newspapers, over the radio, and on Capitol Hill.

The prospect of endless local manipulation of the clocks also made everyone at the ICC miserable. "Its plaintive wail is that States and cities, by juggling their clocks as they please, are making a mockery of the federal law purporting to set up and maintain a standard time system," reported the *Post*. One exasperated inspector for the commission told the newspaper, "I guess the railroads are about the only ones who pay any attention to the standard time zones any more."

Business and commerce did not promote reliable national standards; what was convenient to one was inconvenient to another. And uniformity was often the enemy of competition. In the fall of 1936, a *Post* editorial fondly recalled the days of old, "when a man traveled from coast to coast, [and] every day or so he realized he had covered enough ground to knock off another hour. Crossing the ocean, part of his morning ritual on shipboard is to check the clock by the purser's desk." But American Airlines had altered that routine and challenged everyone's sense of time. All clock times, from Eastern Daylight Saving to Pacific Standard, were "encompassed in a single transcontinental flight aboard the American Mercury, within the space of 15 hours."

Time was leaving the railroads behind. The future was in the air. By 1928, the *New York Times* could confidently declare, "The ether is the nation's alarm clock and the radio stations have taken over the custodianship of the hour." Bongs, bells, and beeps transmitted by commercial broadcasters to receivers in homes across the country had become the signal for setting clocks and watches to the correct time. Since 1912, the U.S. Navy had been broadcasting the mean time every hour from Arlington, Virginia, but with the rapid development of commercial radio after 1920, a new citizen's band had been created. Radio promised the formation of a national assembly whose entire membership could be addressed or informed or entertained at a single moment by a single person.

Radio was able to collapse the time zones. In an emergency, or on the whim of a corporation or politician, a radio broadcast could create a simultaneous moment of awe or fear or outrage in Atlanta and Seattle. Live radio broadcasts were potent evidence of the actuality of Universal Time. A storm or an assassination or a record-breaking dash happened at one time on one particular day, no matter where you were when it happened. You could hear about it—and by 1939, with the advent of national television broadcasts, watch it—as it happened. In these dramatic moments, local time was subordinated to Universal Time.

Radio was the most powerful weapon in the arsenal of the country's most powerful commercial and political interests, and Daylight Saving was almost uniformly despised by broadcasters. It wreaked havoc with radio schedules, licensing guidelines, and the habits of the listening audience. Within a single time zone—often within a single county—weather reports, transportation updates, and headline news could not be properly timed. Local radio stations could not segregate their signals to send out the 7:00 news first to radios in towns with Daylight Saving Time, and an hour later to those without Daylight ordinances. Simply announcing the time was a dicey proposition.

Live programming produced by regional broadcasters, including prayer services and "church hours," often had to be staged twice, once for Daylight stations and once for Standard Time stations. The physical-fitness coaches who led the popular morning "setting-up" exercise programs did double their normal number of jumping jacks and toe touches during Daylight Saving months. And radio stations with restricted daytime licenses that were headquartered in cities without Daylight Saving appeared to be off the air entirely to listeners who woke up and turned on their radios in a neighboring town or city whose clocks had been advanced that spring.

Although technological limits made early broadcasts strictly local or regional phenomena, by 1928 the Federal Radio Commission was sorting through various proposals for national broadcasting rights. Despite its power to create universal moments, however, national broadcasting did not propel the nation toward the adoption of the twenty-four-hour Universal Time clock. Instead, broadcasters discovered the commercial advantages of delayed and prerecorded programming.

Radio retained its capacity to provoke simultaneous experience, but broadcasting principally developed and profited by a divide-and-conquer strategy. Instead of erasing time-zone boundaries, commercial radio reinforced them, doling out after-dinner programs of music and comedy to each time zone over four consecutive hours. National broadcasting created a standard evening, a set of identical experiences to be lived at the appropriate local time. At 7:00 P.M. Pacific Time, a person in Los Angeles could look forward to the same preprogrammed evening that had been enjoyed by a person who was going to bed at 10:00 P.M. Eastern Time in Philadelphia. This uniformity appealed to Americans.

Warren G. Harding installed the first radio in the White House, in 1922. A few months later, the first radio debate in history was broadcast from Washington, D.C. The president did not participate. The debate featured students from the National University Law School.

It aired live on 23 May 1922. The decision of the judges was not announced during the broadcast. Listeners had to decide for themselves which side had won. The topic was Daylight Saving.

Harding and his successors did speak to the nation over the airwaves, but it was Franklin Roosevelt who learned to play the radio for all it was worth, perfecting the modern art of intimate mass communication. The first of his thirty "fireside chats" was broadcast to the entire nation at 10:00 P.M. Eastern Standard Time on 12 March 1933, one week after his inauguration. Roosevelt explained his rationale for closing the nation's banks for ten days, an emergency measure euphemistically referred to as a "bank holiday." This impromptu holiday was the first of many initiatives and reforms Roosevelt pursued without regard for the established conventions of time and timekeeping.

Among the most controversial and profound of these was the National Recovery Administration, which proposed minimum hourly pay rates for various professions and attempted to establish daily and weekly limits on the number of hours people should be expected to work for their wages. The initial standards were ultimately found to be unconstitutional, but the administration persisted, and its revisions and adaptations led to the codification of the eight-hour industrial working day and the establishment of a nationwide minimum wage. As a result, the hour became a fixed standard for measuring the relative value of work and the relative merits of workers. By defining the average, or mean working day, the administration also defined the nonworking day, creating a reliable, uniform expectation of late-afternoon and evening leisure time for millions of Americans. In effect, the Social Security Act enlarged this idea and applied it to the life span, democratizing the expectation of a prolonged period of retirement.

Roosevelt commanded unprecedented authority over the commercial interests of the country, applying federally regulated controls to the daily conduct of banking and business, and promoting recovery and growth by stimulating productivity in every sector of the economy. To the consternation of many of his greatest supporters, during his first ten years in office, he never applied his considerable powers of persuasion to passage of a national Daylight Saving law.

It was a significant omission. Roosevelt surely had no aversion to federal programs; in its first three years, his administration created more than fifty new government agencies. He was absolutely unafraid to meddle in affairs of the clock and calendar. And Daylight's most persistent lobbyist, the Chamber of Commerce, was welcome in the White House. Indeed, in 1939, the president presented the Chamber of Commerce, the representative of retail merchants across the country, with one of the biggest and strangest holiday gifts in history.

In the summer of 1939, in the hopes of boosting holiday retail sales by extending the Christmas shopping period, Roosevelt suddenly decided to change the date of Thanksgiving Day. He moved it back by a week. Of course, Americans had long debated the origin of this holiday, when it had initially been celebrated, who had hosted the first feast, and exactly what had been on the menu. However, the day for celebrating had been fixed in 1863 by Abraham Lincoln, who declared that Thanksgiving Day was always the last Thursday of November. So it was until 1939. Roosevelt shoved the holiday back from 30 November to 23 November, mucking up every calendar in the country, all school and university vacations, and unleashing a tremendous editorial exchange of misinformation about Native Americans, Pilgrims, wild turkeys, cranberry sauce, and the traditions of timekeeping.

In 1939, Franklin and Eleanor Roosevelt celebrated Thanksgiving Day on 23 November in Warm Springs, Georgia, at a health spa the president often visited. The editor of the *Warm Springs Mirror*, Edward Stout, later told the Associated Press he was working on a plan for a better birthday for President Roosevelt, who was born in January. "Too cold to celebrate," he said. "Move it up a few months, to

June, maybe." When the Roosevelts returned to Washington the following week, Mrs. Roosevelt denied reports that she and her husband would be celebrating the holiday a second time, on 30 November.

Many Americans did celebrate on 30 November, however. In the absence of a national law, the change of date for Thanksgiving had to be effected on a state-by-state basis. Some states went with the new date, and some stuck to the old, which led to a patchwork of holiday celebrations across the country and often made it impossible to assemble parents and their college-age children and a roasted turkey in one room on the same day. The confusion was especially hard on college football fans, as holiday games between traditional rivals were not all played on one day. And each year, the states were forced to choose again, which often led to last-minute decisions and reversals. In 1941, the *New York Times* tally was as confounding as its annual Daylight Saving survey:

> Eleven states, including Massachusetts, where turkey day started, have changed their minds since 1940. Two-thirds of the nation will go along with President Roosevelt in celebrating Nov. 20, the date he has named as Thanksgiving Day. The other third will carve its turkey on Nov. 27, the old-fashioned, last-Thursday-in-the-month sanctioned by tradition. Since last year, when sixteen States stuck to tradition, at least five states have switched into line with the new version, but six others have gone back.

In 1939, the first year of the Thanksgiving split, the London *Times* reported that the confusion had a depressing effect on the entire American economy because it created interruptions in normal commerce for two consecutive weeks. The changed date never did increase retail business. A survey conducted by the commissioner of commerce in New York City showed that 77 percent of retail stores had experienced adverse effects on sales during the 1940 Christmas shopping season. In May 1941, Roosevelt decided to endorse Lincoln's old holiday policy; in 1942, the entire nation celebrated Thanksgiving on the last Thursday of November.

In the meantime, back in Georgia, the ICC had moved the boundary of the Eastern Time Zone. Long divided by Eastern and Central Time, the state was made wholly Eastern in 1941. Farmers in western Georgia—a state that had refused even emergency Daylight Saving measures—received the year-round benefits of Daylight Saving, which golfers in Boston, New York, and Chicago enjoyed only during the war years.

Alabama's eastern border became the edge of Central Time. Unfortunately for Alabama's neighbor to the south, the new boundary kept the Florida panhandle in Central Time, while the rest of Florida ran on Eastern Time. When residents of eastern Kentucky and Tennessee saw Georgia's clocks permanently spring forward, they asked for the same consideration, but they were turned down, as was a proposal from Tennessee for a simplification of the time-zone system. According to the *New York Times*, the director of the Chattanooga Chamber of Commerce suggested that all states east of the Mississippi River be included in the Eastern Time Zone once and for all. Arthur V. Snell figured the remaining three zones could be condensed into two, divided by the Rocky Mountain watershed.

It probably would have made sense for the Interstate Commerce Commission to gather up all its strength and shove half the country into the Eastern Time Zone. Instead, the ICC continued to arbitrate requests on an annual basis until the logic of the zones was so utterly convoluted that a reluctant Congress was forced to reconsider its original concept of Standard Time. This did not happen until 1966. By then, the ICC had approved thirty-five changes to the Standard Time zones. It had rejected seven. All forty-two of the proposed changes involved westward movements of existing boundaries; that is, all were petitions for inclusion in a more easterly zone. The states that had rejected Daylight Saving were now begging for Daylight Saving.

Chapter Eight

Men of the Hour

Time is a changeable ally.
—WINSTON CHURCHILL, 1940

In the first few months of 1941, members of President Franklin Delano Roosevelt's administration began to make public statements about the need for the nation to readopt Daylight Saving. World War II had been officially under way since the invasion of Poland in September 1939, which had prompted Great Britain and France to declare war on Germany. Many people in the United States, and a good number of their elected representatives, still did not consider an American declaration of war necessary or inevitable. In February 1941, however, Secretary of the Interior Harold Ickes told the *New York Times* that Daylight Saving was needed "now that we are at war; I mean to say, now that we are preparing our country for national defense." By March, Congress was entertaining national Daylight legislation.

That summer, Secretary Ickes repeated his recommendation and also called for a ban on large electrical signs and nighttime baseball.

The Office of Production Management issued a report detailing the economic and industrial benefits of Daylight Saving, which was already in effect in most nations on both sides of the war, including Britain, France, Denmark, Portugal, Germany, Italy, and Canada. When Colonel William Knox, secretary of the navy, testified before Congress about the need for national Daylight Saving, the London *Times* cited his insistence that "the first and most critical duty was to maintain communications between the United States, Great Britain, and Russia across the North Atlantic."

Coordination was a challenge for the military; it was an impossibility for the civilian populations. By 1941, thanks to Joseph Stalin, timekeepers in Russia had lost track of Greenwich Mean Time, and this Russian problem went unnoticed until the end of the century. Meanwhile, Great Britain had gotten a little carried away with the advancing of its clocks, evidence of Winston Churchill's lifelong passion for Daylight Saving. And long before America found itself on the brink of war, Franklin Roosevelt had demonstrated his willingness to complicate America's traditional sense of working days, holidays, and all things hourly.

In the summer of 1941, there were two specific questions for Americans to consider. Should the entire nation be required to spring forward in 1942? If so, should Daylight Saving Time be effective for five, six, seven, or twelve months of the year?

The debate in Congress and in the press shaped up as a rematch between old rivals; it was basically the farmers versus the retailers. Robert Garland of Pittsburgh suggested a compromise. This was newsworthy; by 1941, Garland was "regarded as the 'father of daylight saving time' in the United States," according to the *New York Times*. An industrialist and longtime president of the Pittsburgh Chamber of Commerce, Garland was credited with putting Daylight Saving at the top of the agenda of the National Chamber of Commerce before World War I. Two decades later, in the months before America entered World War II, Garland again advocated for national Daylight Saving, but only for the summer months. "I think daylight time is a hardship in Winter months. There's no sense to it," he told a reporter for the *Times* on 15 July 1941. The reporter noted that "Mr. Garland added quickly that he didn't think President Roosevelt 'intended to seek year-round daylight time.'"

That same day, Congress received a communication from President Roosevelt explaining the "need for the establishment in various parts, or all, of the country of year-round daylight-saving time." The president also requested the authority to advance the clocks where he saw fit by as much as two hours, for as many months as he deemed necessary. Roosevelt's proposal was bolstered by optimistic math—an anticipated saving of 736,282,000 kilowatt hours of electricity every year—but it also arrived with a new logical twist. Daylight Saving, he argued, would assist defense-related industries and reduce "peak loads" by delaying the demand for streetlights, home lights, and electricity for cooking until after civilian industries had shut down for the day.

The farmers were still not impressed, and there was resistance from other quarters, as well. The country had endured a decade of economic sacrifice, and it had not yet fully recovered from the impact of the Depression. Many Americans were willing to do their part to bolster the nation's defenses, but America was not at war with anyone. And more than twenty years after the national law had been repealed, Daylight Saving still enjoyed a reputation as the premier example of congressional folly and the federal government's arrogance. Indeed, by September 1941, all "appeals for sacrifices from Washington have almost seemed plans for confusion," complained a columnist for *The Nation:*

First was that program to save kilowatts for making aluminum, which began after the long drought in the South. It resulted in voluntary adoption of daylight-saving time in rural states which had not had it before; but the daylight saving began after torrential rains had come and hydroelectric plants were spilling surplus water over their dams. Also, people found that Washington, D.C., stayed on standard time, which may have been all right from the power point of view but did not help the public reaction.... Then we began to collect aluminum... but the men in charge [in cities and towns] seemed almost deliberately taught that the government did not know what it was doing, and the system of collection was changed by telegram from Washington in the middle of the campaign... a local triumph over national confusion. Then, gasoline; it began with a failure, even a rush to greater consumption. Washington instituted a sort of race to the tanks by a program of indefinite reductions accompanied by threats of uncertain rationing.... Not only was petroleum not saved, but public confidence in Washington's good sense was lost.

In this climate, there was little reason to believe the Congress would dare to inflict year-round Daylight Saving on the entire nation. Although polling since 1937 by the American Institute of Public Opinion had consistently shown a majority of Americans in favor of summertime Daylight Saving, as late as June 1941, more than 60 percent of Americans continued to express disapproval for the year-round plan.

The controversy persisted into the winter, until the attack on Pearl Harbor. "The Japanese struck Hawaii at 7:55 A.M. Sunday, December 7, Honolulu time; it was 10:25 A.M. Sunday, Pacific Standard Time, in San Francisco; it was 1:25 P.M. Sunday, Eastern Standard Time, in Washington," recounted the *Washington Post*. "In Britain, the Sunday sun had set. In Tokyo, the daybreak of Monday, December 8, was approaching." On 8 January 1942, the Senate gave the president the authority he had requested over the nation's clocks; a week later, the House did the same. And just one month later, on 9 February, Americans sprang forward for an unspecified period of Daylight Saving, which had a new, purpose-specific name. According to the *New York Times,* "Stephen T. Early, White House press secretary, announced the president's decision to call the new system 'war time,' since, commented Mr. Early, 'that's what it is.'"

The British continued to call it Summer Time. "It is one of the paradoxes of history," wrote Winston Churchill, "that we should owe the boon of summer time, which gives every year to the people of this country between 160 and 170 hours more daylight leisure, to a war which plunged Europe into darkness." He was thinking of World War I.

It was 1934, five years before he became prime minister in the wake of Neville Chamberlain's resignation, when Churchill wrote, "A Silent Toast to William Willett," the father of modern Daylight Saving. Churchill was still charmed by the benefits afforded by the simple manipulation of the clocks, and he was still smarting a bit from the rebukes he had endured on Willett's behalf more than twenty-five years earlier. "I was one of the earliest supporters of Daylight Saving," Churchill wrote, calling the moral arguments against it "indeed, absurd," and remembering that "the most extraordinary criticism of all concerned restaurants . . . that people liked to dine late, and that ladies preferred artificial light." He was more than a little surprised that most European nations had given up on Daylight Saving after 1919 and that the same arguments against it prevailed year after year. "One marvels that so feeble a case should have been sustained so long."

In France, Daylight Saving had become the absinthe of public policy. Some people were, like Churchill, instantly besotted; many were intrigued enough to try it, but never acquired a taste for it. Others found it intolerably bitter, and a few people refused to touch the stuff as a matter of principle. By 1920, the rural population of France had spit it out. Paris and other major cities continued to favor Daylight Saving, typically justifying their habit as a coal-saving measure. But in 1921, people in the eastern regions of France were complaining that Daylight Saving forced them onto German time— an intolerable fate—and people in the western regions, "where the sun's time is nearly an hour later than Paris, complain equally bitterly that under the act one must have his luncheon at what is only about 10 o'clock according to the sun," reported the *New York Times*.

France's former prime minister, Paul Painlevé, suggested the adoption of clocks with three hands to track both official time and local sun time, and then the miners demanded regional exemptions. In 1923, Parisian doctors weighed in with statistical evidence. Despite a 50 percent increase in the city's population since 1913, they pointed out that murders and suicides in the capital city had fallen during that decade from an annual total of almost 1,200 to 800. This they credited to Daylight's ameliorative effect on nervous tension. And in the first year of Daylight Saving, the number of deaths attributable to tuberculosis had dropped from more than 9,000 to well below 7,000. For their efforts, the doctors won a temporary compromise from their countrymen. On 1 April 1923, the *New York Times* reported, "the French Cabinet made the remarkable decision today that the time would remain the same, but that everyone and everything in France, between April 28 and Nov. 3, should start and stop a half-hour earlier." Soon, France followed the example of its continental neighbors and gave it up.

Every year, a few new experiments were launched with Daylight Saving—Belgium and Spain tried it more than once; Canadian cities and provinces annually divided and redivided themselves over it after the nationwide policy was shelved in 1919; Australia, Argentina, and Brazil all saw some reason to put it to the test. Even El Salvador—a nearly equatorial nation, whose summer and winter days did not vary dramatically in length and, thus, was unlikely to experience a dramatic saving—succumbed to the Daylight spirit in 1938, though the legislation was revoked four months after it was introduced.

There is no apparent rational explanation for England's singular attachment to Daylight Saving. Unlike most European nations, the British island lies mostly west of its appointed time-zone meridian, but so do Iceland, Portugal, and any other number of nations, including Ireland, where Daylight was resisted by farmers and Catholic clergy as an insult to home rule, even during World War II. Like most of England, most major West Coast cities in the United States were located in the western half of their Standard Time Zone, but none of them had adopted Daylight Saving by 1940.

Indeed, many loyal subjects of the crown had not taken to it immediately. In 1909, during a reading of the Daylight Saving Act in Parliament, "witticisms were freely indulged in, and the House was in a mood to be amused," reported the London *Times*. "There was a good deal of laughter when Sir F. Banbury suavely inquired what was to become of the sundials in the country, and impressed on the supporters of the bill that ladies would not dine by daylight." In response, the young president of the Board of Trade, Winston Churchill, "pleaded almost passionately for the change that had been advocated, declaring that it demanded respectful consideration." The bill was again rejected, but Churchill "prophesied that a grateful posterity would raise statues in honour of Mr. Willett and decorate them with sunflowers on the longest day of the year."

Every year after 1916, England debated and eventually saved daylight. Finally, in 1925, Parliament passed a permanent law, which made the summer ritual of advancing the clocks an annual event. The next spring, a small holding of land, Petts Wood in Chiselhurst, was set aside as a public park in honor of William Willett. Deep inside the wood, Willett's efforts were memorialized in an inscription on the base of a granite sundial.

Success has one thousand fathers, and failure is an orphan, so in America, Daylight Saving has had five or six fathers and one mother.

In 1919, the *New York Times* dubbed New York Senator William M. Calder "the Father of Daylight Saving because he introduced the bill which brought about nation-wide daylight saving." There were other contenders for the crown—notably, Congressman William Borland, the Kansas City Democrat who sponsored the Daylight bill in the House of Representatives. But the claims of these lawmakers faded with the short-lived national legislation, and for more than a decade, Ben Franklin was regularly awarded the dubious distinction. Franklin's name had bipartisan appeal. For proponents, it seemed to imply a distinguished lineage for Daylight Saving; for opponents, Franklin's satiric 1784 proposal for conserving candle wax and tallow proved that, from the start, the scheme had been a joke.

But in August 1934, Marcus Marks died, and the *New York Times* awarded the first president of the National Daylight Saving Association the honor of being "the acknowledged leader in the daylight-saving movement." Marks had been a beloved crusader in the Manhattan campaign, but he was never celebrated by the rest of the country. Fifteen years earlier, testifying before Congress on behalf of Daylight Saving, Marks had sounded imperious and effete. When a sympathetic congressman from Tennessee assured him that he was doing his best to preserve the national legislation, Marks thanked the legislator and added, "I would positively weep if it were changed." It was just the sort of sentiment Daylight's opponents expected to hear from a wealthy, retired manufacturer, a trustee of the Carnegie Endowment for International Peace with a fancy home on Fifth Avenue.

Marcus Marks was not given a chance to explain why he might weep. In New York, he had founded the Educational Alliance and a "preventorium" for impoverished families and children—most of them first-generation Americans—threatened by tuberculosis. Exercise and exposure to sunlight—otherwise known as leisure—were the cheapest and most reliable means of inoculating this population against communicable diseases. In its posthumous tribute, the *New*

York Times not only ushered Marks onto the throne previously reserved for Ben Franklin; the newspaper highlighted his altruistic spirit, calling the newly proclaimed father of Daylight Saving an exemplar "of the civic virtues which were claimed by Pericles for the Athenians."

The coronation of Marcus Marks was challenged in 1937, upon the death of another leading citizen of New York—Mrs. Marcus Marks, a champion of universal suffrage, birth control, and the Equal Rights Amendment. "While the daylight-saving movement has been accredited to her husband," eulogized the editors at *Equal Rights,* "it was she who, having read of a similar idea in a paper in Germany, started the daylight-saving movement which was worked out by Mr. Marks in the United States."

Perhaps wisely, the *New York Times* avoided the Marks family altogether when Daylight Saving became a fashionable editorial subject in the run-up to World War II. In addition to the domestic squabble, Mr. and Mrs. Marks had an international liability. In 1928, the *New York Times* had reported on the couple's trip to Rome, where "Marks explained the working of daylight saving in the United States to Premier Mussolini," and predicted it would be the next Fascist reform:

> The Premier was interested when Mr. Marks told him of the saving in bills for gas, coal, and electricity effected by setting the clocks ahead, as well as the greater period of daylight recreation for the workers.... "Mussolini is the most magnetic man I ever met and the most interesting," Mr. Marks said. His wife and daughter, who were present at the interview, expressed the same opinion.

So in 1941, the *Times* announced that Robert Garland was "regarded as father of daylight saving time in the United States." This is how Robert Garland regarded himself. In 1927, Garland had published the pamphlet "Ten Years of Daylight Saving," in which he not only named his Pittsburgh Chamber of Commerce "the first commercial body in the entire country to present the subject to the Chamber of Commerce of the United States for its consideration," but also produced photographs of his collection of three fountain pens—the pens used by Speaker of the House Champ Clark, Vice President Thomas Marshall, and President Woodrow Wilson to sign the 1918 national legislation.

Garland's title did not go unchallenged. In July 1941, a letter from Warren Marks, the son of Marcus Marks, appeared in the *Times* under the headline "Paternity of Daylight Saving." The younger Marks recounted his father's years of work on behalf of the time change, including private conferences with President Wilson. "From the time the Daylight Saving Law was put into effect my father was regarded as the father of daylight saving," he asserted. Warren Marks didn't mention his mother or Mussolini; nor did he challenge the provenance of Robert Garland's fountain pens. He did, however, make a definitive claim for paternity. "My father, the late Marcus Marks, former President of the Borough of Manhattan, inaugurated daylight saving at 2 A.M. on March 31, 1918. Previous to that, he had created the phrase 'daylight saving' after reading about 'summer time' in Europe."

It is difficult to establish the paternity of an idea with any certainty. But someone in the Marks household certainly forgot to tell someone else that the phrase *daylight saving,* like so many other English words, was coined in England. William Willett's 1907 pamphlet, "A Waste of Daylight," occasioned its birth, and the term immediately achieved currency. Indeed, by 1908, according to the London *Times,* the "Daylight Saving Act" had already achieved infamy.

In 1942, Franklin Roosevelt settled the question. After he signed the "War Time" law, he ordered that his pen be sent to Robert Garland. It was a vindication for the man whom Daylight's early opponents had painted as a rich industrialist who cared more about city folk and their leisure than he did about traditional values—a false portrait based largely on facts.

As president of a remarkably profitable electrical-conduit manufacturing business, Garland enjoyed a thirty-year term on the Pittsburgh City Council and became a relentless lobbyist on behalf of
manufacturers and merchants through the Chamber of Commerce.
He was also an immigrant. He'd arrived from Ireland at the age of
fifteen and worked as a clerk in a steel mill, and with the money he
saved from his wages, he started his own business when he was
thirty-one. He was a devout worshipper at the Calgary Episcopal
Church in Pittsburgh, and in his memory, the processional hymn on
the April Sunday of the clock change is always the same:

> *Months of due succession, days of lengthening light,*
> *Hours and passing moments praise thee in their flight.*
> *Brightness of the morning, sky and fields and sea,*
> *Vanquisher of darkness, bring their praise to Thee.*

Shortly before his death in 1949, Garland was asked about Daylight Saving. He didn't mention the war or commerce or kilowatts.
"Only Man is stupid enough to deprive himself of an extra hour of
sun by sticking to a rigid system of time," he told the *New York
Times*. "When I think of all the youngsters—and oldsters, too—
enjoying that extra hour in the evening, I feel I really have accomplished something worthwhile in my life."

While he was clearing up the paternity question, Franklin Roosevelt
could have resolved a much thornier issue in the Daylight debate.
Before 1941, it had seemed impossible to ascertain whether Daylight
Saving was an effective means of conserving fuel. Statistics had
been manipulated and misquoted on both sides of the debate. The
utility companies had often denied that they were opposed to Daylight Saving or that their revenues were affected by it. The most
compelling evidence had to be inferred. A national Daylight Saving
law would have pleased many of Roosevelt's most loyal political and

commercial constituencies, but the White House never proposed one. Roosevelt must have had a clear indication that national Daylight Saving would cut fuel demand and, thus, compromise his fundamental goal of stimulating productivity and consumption in the aftermath of the Depression.

The president's initial request to Congress for War Time—that is, year-round Daylight Saving—confirmed this inference. Roosevelt told Congress that the regional and municipal utilities had "reported that daylight saving time might seriously cut their revenues and jeopardize the interest and amortization payments on bonded indebtedness." Their anxiety about diminishing fuel consumption persisted even as the administration stoked the fires of the largest industrial war-production effort in history. Evidently, Daylight Saving reduced the demand for fuel.

In 1942, the nation was pushed ahead onto War Time. Manufacturers revised their production schedules to take advantage of a daily 2 percent reduction in peak-load demand, and the federal government anticipated a national saving of 0.75 billion kilowatt hours, energy that could be diverted to the military buildup. Until 1945, America's clocks remained one hour ahead of Standard Time— whatever that meant in a particular city or region by 1942.

Timekeeping in the rest of the world had become a potluck affair, as the *Washington Post* pointed out the day before War Time took effect:

> Daylight saving time, double summer time, Hitler time, and Tojo time have scrambled the time zones of the globe. . . . At the same moment, Americans may some day be fighting a Monday battle in Europe or Africa and a Tuesday battle in the southwest Pacific. The same naval flotilla might even fight a mid-Pacific engagement in two days at once.

Although their primary duties were governed by twenty-four-hour Military Time, which was the same in Washington, D.C., Berlin,

Moscow, London, and Tokyo, soldiers inevitably developed a familiarity with the local time of the countries in which they were stationed. To prevent this, and to inculcate the citizens of conquered nations to the German notion of unification, Hitler's commanders imposed German time as they moved through Europe. It didn't always work. Denmark had adopted Daylight Saving for the war and planned to turn its clocks back in mid-August, when the total amount of daylight in that northerly country began to decrease noticeably. On the appointed fall-back day in 1940, the German occupiers announced that Danish citizens were not allowed to turn back their clocks. The Danish farmers made such a ruckus, however, that the Nazis were forced to negotiate, and Denmark ended up only half an hour ahead of normal. The French had resisted Daylight Saving at the start of the war, but they failed to resist the German army, which meant that they were officially on "Hitler time" by 1941. The Vichy departments, in a pale show of patriotism, stuck to the old French time, two hours behind the Berlin-based Daylight Saving Time of the German occupiers, according to the *Washington Post*.

While American citizens were just getting accustomed to War Time, Winston Churchill prepared the British to leap ahead of their new Allies. He called for a double dose of Summer Time. Having adopted year-round Daylight Saving in 1939, Great Britain advanced its clocks again in May 1941. Six months a year, the British were two hours ahead of Greenwich Mean Time, the standard they'd sold to the rest of the world. The value of this extra extra hour as a fuel-conservation measure was hotly debated, but Double Summer Time was hailed as a boon to industrial productivity and public safety. With two hours of morning light shifted to the afternoons, freight yards and docks could operate well into the evenings, and industrial plants were able to arrange two complete shifts during daylight hours. And later and later twilights meant that people could commute home from work, eat their evening meals, and even enjoy their after-dinner radio programs before the skies darkened and the likelihood of air raids increased. The blackout conditions that persisted in

London for five years made Daylight Saving both a life preserver and a lifesaver.

Russia did not adopt Daylight Saving during World War II. This made for three different national timekeeping policies among the three most important Allied nations. The Russian anomaly was the source of some consternation among clock watchers in this country. Most commentators concluded that Russia had problems enough with its eleven Standard Time zones. "When it is noon in Moscow, it is nearly midnight in Siberia," the *Washington Post* reminded its readers. "Moscow, which normally sees the dawn of a new day eight hours ahead of New York, will have her clocks set only seven hours ahead after the [Americans] change over to War Time."

In fact, Moscow normally should have been only seven hours ahead of New York. But for most of the twentieth century, it was difficult for outsiders to ascertain exactly what the Russians were up to. After the 1917 Bolshevik revolution, the provisional government had temporarily adopted Daylight Saving "for the purpose of economy in the consumption of fuel," according to the *New York Times*. In this way, the Russians were ahead of their time, and though the Bolsheviks soon abandoned Daylight Saving, the Russians spent most of the century ahead of their time, thanks to Joseph Stalin.

Stalin reinstated Daylight Saving in the spring of 1930. He had launched the first of his brutal Five-Year plans in 1928, and he became a merciless manipulator of time. In 1929, he outlawed the seven-day week and disposed of the various European, Christian, and regional calendars in use, replacing them with a system of five-day weeks. This unusual timekeeping approach failed, and in 1931, the USSR officially adopted a six-day week, which provided Soviet workers with one day off every week instead of the customary two-day weekend. February was standardized into a thirty-day month, and whenever a month with thirty-one days rolled around, workers were rewarded with an extra day of work. This system worked until 1940. Soon after the German invasion of its territory, the USSR stopped manufacturing its own weeks, went to war, and permanently adopted the standard seven-day week.

After the spring of 1930, Stalin never again ordered the nation to spring forward. For the duration of World War II and the much longer Cold War that ensued, the Supreme Soviet was one of the few national assemblies that did not compel its citizens to manipulate their clocks. So it was a surprise to Soviet citizens and foreigners when, in March 1981, the Associated Press reported a blitz of publicity in Moscow that began with a bold headline in *Pravda*: "Change Your Clocks on Time, Dear Comrades!" The Russians were going to spring forward again. The Tass news agency repeatedly assured citizens it was not an April Fool's joke and predicted that the clock change would save more than 2 billion kilowatt hours of electricity. "Soviet medics," according to United Press International, "confirmed that the introduction of summer time answers the seasonal changes in the biorhythm of the human organism."

All eleven time zones survived the change and safely fell back in the autumn, but after a few years of advancing their clocks in the spring, several Soviet republics began to resent Daylight Saving. Estonia, which had been forced onto Moscow time in the 1940s, announced its intention to reestablish "solar time." Latvia and Lithuania shared a time zone with Estonia, and soon followed its lead. The empire was breaking apart.

In March 1991, the *Wall Street Journal* reported the surprising news that the Kremlin had ordered the nation not to turn its clocks ahead that spring. More surprising was the rationale for the government decision:

> Soviet officials admit they haven't kept the correct time for 61 years, blaming a Stalin-era error for failing to turn clocks back an hour when they should have been. Thus, the U.S.S.R. is scrapping daylight-saving time this month, but clocks will "fall back" an hour this fall.... Estonia, Latvia, Lithuania, and Moldavia will move their

clocks ahead. But Tadzhikistan, parts of Kazakstan, and other regions will set their clocks back an hour to organize daylight hours better.

The *Toronto Star* could not get a clear explanation from any of the "red-faced Soviet officials" about Stalin's failure to make Russian clocks fall back in 1930. Neither could residents of Moscow. Nor could they understand why the government had directed them to do nothing. It seemed obvious to a lot of people that they should turn back the time to fix the problem. A *Pravda* headline asked, "Are We Going to Move Our Hands?" The answer was provided by the *Evening Moscow:* "On March 31, one should not move the hands of the clock ahead, but go to bed as usual."

In the fall of 1991, Russia's clocks were set back by an hour. For the first time in more than sixty years, Moscow was seven hours ahead of New York, where it belonged, according to the zone times established in 1884. As the Soviet Union disintegrated, commentators throughout the West exploited the timely irony. Stalin's goof became an irresistible illustration of the inevitable failure of Soviet-style central planning. That fall, the *National Review* printed a version of these events cast as a parable, which concluded that Stalin "forgot to return to regular time. For 61 years the Soviet Union has been living on false time. . . . Everyone agrees that Communism as a belief system is dead; but what intellectual implications does that have?"

In truth, by 1991, the phrase *false time* was redundant. But one clear implication of the Russian fiasco was the irrelevance of one hour of mean time in matters of international war, diplomacy, and trade. The lost hour had not interfered with the making of history. And there was another implication, which was articulated by Louis Marck in a letter to the *New York Times* that autumn. Not only had the Soviets strayed from Standard Time, but the rest of the world had apparently strayed from its habit of checking facts in standard reference books: "To call Moscow's 1930 nonreturn to winter time a mistake rooted in forgetfulness smacks of journalistic license," wrote

Marck. "The time-zone map in the 1974 *Britannica Atlas* simply says that standard time zones are advanced one hour for all of the Soviet Union." Marck implied that Stalin's apparent mistake might have been a sly maneuver. Perhaps Stalin had intended to keep the clocks in the USSR running one hour ahead of mean time on a year-round basis. "I wouldn't bet the Soviets will let their clocks alone next spring," cautioned Marck. "If they did, it would mean the abolition of daylight saving time."

A few months after the Russians settled into their true Mean Time, in December 1991, they noticed something unusual was happening. It was getting dark by 3:00 in the afternoon every day. On 13 January 1992, Tass issued a press release:

> Administrations of 40 Russian provinces have proposed to the Supreme Soviet of Russia to move the Standard Time one hour ahead to prolong the duration of daylight hours in the evening. Russia will change over to so-called Daylight Saving measure from 19 January 1992.... Due to light saving measures abolished in 1991, three billion kilowatt hours of electricity were lost on the territory of the former Soviet Union. To generate that much power, 700 thousand tons of black oil was wasted. With reversion to the Summer Time in Russia, the hands of the clock will be put forward for the second time on the last Sunday of March.... By the end of September Russia will revert to the Winter Time by putting the clock hands back one hour.

It had no real value in the world at large, but the hour that had been lost for sixty years in the pages of the *Britannica* meant something to its original owners. From Ukraine to the Baltic to Siberia, the independent republics formed and reformed themselves over the next decade, frequently recalibrating their Standard Time zones, annually renegotiating their relationships to Greenwich Mean Time, and endlessly reevaluating their seasonally variable affections and disaffections for Daylight Saving. In their attempts to make sense of that hour, the people who had been America's strategic allies for the first half century and its greatest enemies for the second found themselves in an all-American mess.

Every year since 1991, the Duma has been beset by petitions and proposals to abolish Daylight Saving. Every year, the Russians have sprung ahead. Every year, said Vladimir Labinov, production suffers. He wasn't worried about fuel or military preparedness. He was worried about the cows. On the eve of the final autumn clock change of the century, the director of the Agriculture Ministry's time service told the *Moscow Times,* "The cattle lose sleep at the time of the spring change. This means a 5 to 8 percent loss in the season's yield."

Chapter Nine

Out of Uniform

The time is out of joint. O cursed spite
That ever I was born to set it right!
—WILLIAM SHAKESPEARE, 1600

War is hell, but War Time in Wieser, Idaho, was worse. It was August 1942 when the residents of the small town broke rank with the rest of the country and set their clocks back by an hour to Standard Time. The Allies had yet to win a single major victory against the Axis powers; General Montgomery would not defeat Rommel in North Africa until October. The year-round Daylight Saving plan known as War Time had been in effect for just six months, and already there were defectors.

In western Idaho, Wieser, along with neighboring towns in eastern Oregon, was stuck at the distended western edge of the Mountain Time Zone, which normally kept its clocks about forty-five minutes ahead of sun time. War Time meant that Wieser's clocks hit noon when the sun said it was 10:15 A.M. The autumn harvest was approaching, which was reason enough for Wieser to retake some morning sunshine. But the farmers could not defeat War Time by themselves, so in 1942, the residents of Wieser created a class of victims that would haunt Daylight Saving for decades to come—schoolchildren. "Last winter," reported the *Washington Post,* "when war time went into effect, many western Idaho schools had to open at 10 A.M., instead of the customary 9 A.M., so country pupils wouldn't have to leave home for school before daylight." For the next fifty years, communities across the country would attribute many early-morning pedestrian and school bus accidents to the untimely darkness created by Daylight Saving.

War Time in America had many enemies. In the autumn of 1942, the Michigan legislature voted to turn back the state's clocks from Eastern to Central Time, which negated the effect of War Time. Several Michigan cities refused to obey this order, adding to the confusion. Detroit remained on Eastern War Time. According to the *Washington Post,* divided loyalties in Ann Arbor, Bay City, Jackson, and Flint meant that the county courthouse clocks ran one hour behind clocks operated by those Michigan cities. Ohio also went AWOL from War Time, and rural communities in other states began to fall back as well, even before American soldiers were shipped off for the 1944 D-Day invasion. The War Production Board attempted to shore up the domestic time troops with encouraging statistics; it estimated that the annual fuel saving attributable to War Time had turned out to be twice as big as prewar estimates. Nonetheless, by January 1943, Representative William C. Cole of Missouri had introduced national legislation to restore America to "God's Time"—otherwise known as Standard Time.

It would be hard to imagine a more compelling rationale for Daylight Saving than the fate of the free world. Moreover, Franklin Roosevelt stuck to a consistent, year-round time throughout the war years. Thus, War Time had eliminated the biannual clock change—often cited as the primary inconvenience to commerce and the most annoying aspect of Daylight Saving for individuals. And apparently, the plan had worked. By the spring of 1945, the federal government credited War Time with saving more than 5 billion kilowatt hours of electricity.

Reason did not prevail, however. And as the events of 1945 conclusively proved, the Daylight controversy would not be quelled. It persisted through national tragedy and triumph. Roosevelt's untimely death in April 1945 elevated Vice President Harry Truman to the presidency at a critical moment. During his first four months in office, Truman had to negotiate the terms of the German surrender, carry on as commander in chief of the troops in the Pacific, and make the fateful decision to use America's atomic arsenal to decimate Hiroshima and Nagasaki, which altered the course of modern history and, more immediately, impelled the Japanese to surrender in August 1945. Throughout that summer, several congressmen busied themselves and their colleagues by writing and introducing bills to repeal War Time.

The original War Time legislation had stipulated a return to Standard Time within six months of the end of hostilities. But after the Japanese surrendered on 14 August, the prospect of a domestic coal shortage worried several federal agencies, which called for an extension of War Time through the winter of 1945–1946. "Even before the Congress recessed," reported the *New York Times* on 18 August, "the storm broke upon members, and a score of War Time repeal measures piled into the hoppers." In September, War Time was revoked. Clocks around the country fell back into the customary chaos.

The 1945 Gallup poll showed 46 percent of Americans in favor of staying on Standard Time all year. This was only slightly larger than the 42 percent who favored some form of Daylight Saving—either in the summertime (25 percent) or year-round (17 percent). The pollsters did not ask Americans which Standard Time they favored.

In 1946, the state of Virginia decided to eliminate Central Time in its western half by moving the boundary of the Eastern Time

Zone again. This advanced the clocks in all of those cities and towns by one hour. The Interstate Commerce Commission (ICC) officially approved this extension, and shoved parts of North Carolina, Kentucky, and Tennessee onto Eastern Time, as well.

These maneuvers did not resolve the mid-Atlantic time confusion. When Virginia advanced the clocks in its western regions, the state also passed a law banning Daylight Saving, which had been adopted by Norfolk and other eastern Virginia communities. This was a new legal twist. The 1918 federal Standard Time law had specifically granted the local option for Daylight Saving to towns and cities, but it had not anticipated the possibility of a statewide ban, which effectively made the federal law a challenge to a state's rights. Norfolk sprang ahead, eluding the legal complications with a so-called voluntary policy, which was the standard method by which towns and cities exempted themselves from dictates of their state legislatures. And the next year, Virginia's ambivalent neighbors in the District of Columbia adopted summertime Daylight Saving for the first time, creating a larger, regional wrinkle.

With 2.5 million Americans traveling daily by train and another 1.5 million on buses, the variety of local and seasonal times was a recipe for inconvenience. "The long-distance railroads and bus lines operate on standard time," reported the *Washington Post* in 1946, "but most of the bus companies on short-run franchises use Daylight Time. The crazy quilt of time across the country, according to the Interstate Commerce Commission, is driving transcontinental trade to desperation." Not only were timetables unreliable; the watches worn by passengers and transportation employees were often running on different local times. Conducting simple telephone transactions across time zones was also impossible without a detailed, up-to-the-minute tally of local time ordinances. Business travelers attempting to schedule a flight and a day of appointments in neighboring cities were no better off, as the *Washington Post* illustrated by tracking a man with two meetings in Ohio, who asked the airline clerk a simple question: "Is Columbus on daylight saving time or not?"

> The clerk tells him that by law State offices in Ohio are observing eastern standard time, but that some municipalities are on daylight time, and he'll have to look it up. Finally, the clerk announces that Columbus is on Eastern Standard Time. . . . The clerk, after further arduous investigation finds that Indianapolis is on Central Daylight Saving Time. In other words, clocks in Columbus and Indianapolis, which are in different time belts, read the same. . . . The clerk said that the airline she worked for employed 60 information clerks each eight-hour shift to answer an average of 8,000 calls a day. Half of these calls, she said, were made by persons wanting to know what time it was in any one of several hundred cities.

Although by 1950 the Gallup polls showed a slight majority of Americans in favor of summertime Daylight Saving, the number of observant cities had begun to fall, and more than half of the states had no Daylight Saving. Indiana, divided by two time zones, had long used Daylight Saving to make all clocks in the state run together during the summer months. But after the war, Indiana lawmakers passed a ban on Daylight Saving, which guaranteed that clocks in the state would be out of sync all year. In the fall of 1948, voters in Oregon had approved a Daylight Saving referendum, but the legislature passed a subsequent law that made the referendum effective only if the state of California sprang forward. In 1948, California had been forced by a water shortage to advance its clocks to conserve electricity, but as soon as the rains came, the policy was repealed. Then, Oregon banned Daylight Saving. Major cities from Washington, D.C., to Seattle remade their Daylight decisions every year, and the local option encouraged innovation. The California resort city of Palm Springs had a peculiarly local problem. After 3:00 in the afternoon, "Mount San Jacinto, 11,000 feet above sea level, casts an afternoon shadow," reported the *New York Times,* so the city council passed a four-month Daylight Saving policy, which advanced clocks during the winter months.

Across the country, roosters continued to crow at sunrise, rousing the anger of their keepers. Dairy farmers in western Pennsylvania threatened strikes against Daylight Saving cities, and Kentucky farmers went to court in an unsuccessful bid to force Daylighters in Lexington to turn back their clocks. By 1949, the House and the Senate were faced with dozens of new bills filed on behalf of farmers from Louisiana to Iowa seeking to make Standard Time mandatory throughout the year. The Maryland State Grange unanimously endorsed the idea of nationwide Standard Time, and simultaneously launched a campaign for harsher screening of wartime émigrés in the federal government's Displaced Persons program, many of whom were "leaving Maryland farms to seek their fortunes in the city," the grange told the *Washington Post.*

In the spring of 1950, approximately 50 million Americans sprang ahead, while the other 90 million lagged behind. A correspondent for the London *Times* reported on the trouble the Yanks were having: "The railways at their New York stations have added an extra hand, painted red, to their clocks to indicate the new [Daylight] time, hoping in this way to spare their least mathematically minded passengers chagrin."

In the immediate aftermath of the war, many European nations imposed Daylight Saving on their citizens to conserve fuel for national recovery and rebuilding programs. But with the notable exception of Great Britain, Daylight Saving in Europe had become a symbol of the war itself and the humiliation of foreign occupation. Soon after they hung up Mussolini, the Italians shelved Daylight Saving for twenty years. After the French cleared up the debris of the German occupation, they too repealed Daylight Saving and for thirty years refused to readopt it, demurring even at the onset of the worldwide oil shortage in the early 1970s. The city of Berlin had been divided into four occupation zones, and until 1948, the French, British, American, and Soviet occupiers imposed Daylight Saving on the residents. After the Soviet Union divided the city in 1949, the two halves of Berlin were further divided by the distinct timekeeping habits of the Russians and the Germans.

Although the American government could not sell national Daylight to its own citizens, it became Daylight's principal importer all over Asia. The Japanese were forced to advance their clocks every summer until 1951. They were told by the American occupation forces that their 4:30 A.M. summer sunrise was a waste of energy, but most Japanese considered Daylight Saving a punishment that helped the Americans squeeze an extra hour of labor out of work crews, disrupted prayer and exercise routines, and necessitated an extra meal at the end of every extralong day. More than fifty years later, the popular sentiment against Daylight Saving in Japan was still informed by the postwar experience.

The United States also brought Daylight to Chungking, China, along with the military equipment and financial resources the Americans supplied to the Nationalist Chinese. But when the Nationalist leader Chiang Kai-Shek retreated to Taiwan in 1948, Daylight Saving didn't survive on the mainland. The clocks of China fell into the hands of the Communists, who are deservedly famous for their capacity to impose and sustain uniformity. To this day, all of China's many timepieces are perfectly synchronized. Although China's territory encompasses four of the time zones drawn in 1884, there is only one time in China. All of China—an east-west span as broad as the continental United States—uses Beijing Time. Beijing's location relative to the western provinces is quite similar to the relative position of Washington, D.C., and American cities on the West Coast. Thus, when the midwinter sun rises after 7:00 A.M. in Beijing, people in the western provinces do not see sunrise until after 10:00 A.M.

After mainland China shrugged off Daylight Saving and the Soviet Union sealed off North Korea, the American Lieutenant General John Hodge countered by imposing Daylight Saving on Seoul and the rest of South Korea. The citizens of South Korea endured this inconvenience until the end of the brutal war with their former compatriots in the north, but they didn't like it any more than did the Japanese. When the South Koreans established self-government, they abolished Daylight Saving and eschewed the clock change for almost forty years—until the American television networks occupied the country during the 1988 Olympics and found that the hour saved by Daylight Saving served their broadcast plans.

As millions of people around the world and across the United States sought to free themselves from the tyranny of fast time, New York City extended its observance of Daylight Saving from the end of September to the end of October in 1955. The *New York Times* considered this extension a bonus. The editors conceded that Daylight Saving Time was "a symbol by which we deceive ourselves. . . . But it is by symbols, largely, that we live," they rhapsodized, "and D.S.T. is a symbol of vacation, the out-of-doors, and, possibly, young love."

Madison Avenue didn't catch spring fever, however, and in 1956, executives from the National Broadcasting Company and the Columbia Broadcasting System recruited dairy farmers from Chenango County, New York, to join their lobbying efforts against the extension of Daylight Saving. The executives complained to the *New York Times* about "the thousands of dollars it costs the networks to juggle their programs for the benefit of areas where the clocks move up," and the farmers added that it was "no particular help to anyone." When New York City did not relent, the Pennsylvania Railroad decided it would be more economical to join New York than to fight it. The railroad announced its intention to adopt Daylight Saving Time in all its passenger information. However, the beleaguered chairman of the ICC

reminded the ailing railroad that it was required to stick to Standard
Time. In fact, for forty years, the ICC had enforced Standard Time
for the convenience of the railroads.

Seeing no end to the confusion, Representative Harley O. Staggers of West Virginia resubmitted a bill calling on Congress to establish uniform dates for the beginning and end of Daylight Saving
anywhere it was adopted, an idea he had been peddling without success since 1949. But Congress did nothing. And in 1957, Wisconsin
voters surprised the nation twice—by turning out in record numbers
for a springtime referendum and by endorsing statewide Daylight
Saving. A few days later, the Minnesota legislature pushed that
state's clocks ahead for the first time. Kentucky responded in 1958 by
threatening anyone who publicly displayed any time but Standard
Time with a fine or imprisonment. And finally, in 1959, someone
tossed a bright new idea into Tennessee's fifteen-year stew of altered
time zones and wildcat clock changes, and the pot finally boiled over.

The ICC was called in to Nashville. As the *New York Times*
explained, it was a complicated mission:

> In the course of the [fifteen-year] controversy, voters in a number of
> Tennessee cities approved Daylight Time for the summer months.
> Then the proponents of Standard Time appealed to the legislature
> and a law was enacted requiring observance of the time prescribed
> by the I.C.C. City areas got around this by adopting "voluntary"
> Daylight Time, although government offices remained on Standard
> Time. A new appeal to the legislature won another law making it a
> misdemeanor for business establishments to have clocks on any-
> thing but Standard Time. A counter move took the issue to the
> State Supreme Court, which ruled that fixing of the time was a
> proper exercise of the state's police powers.

Enter the Nashville Chamber of Commerce. If they couldn't
have Daylight Saving, the merchants wanted to drag the tattered

western boundary of the Eastern Time Zone further west to include middle Tennessee, which was Central Time territory. The chamber asserted the convenience of commerce in Nashville would be better served if the city were aligned with the major East Coast cities.

In the fall of 1959, Nashville was informed that it was not going anywhere. The ICC rejected the city's bid for Eastern Time. Eventually, Nashville did get summer Daylight Saving Time. More significantly, the whole Tennessee experience gave the ICC such a powerful migraine that the regulatory agency was brought to its knees, where it proceeded to beg for mercy. On 8 January 1960, the *New York Times* announced, "The Interstate Commerce Commission told Congress today that it wants to get rid of an old headache—the regulation of the nation's standard time zone boundaries." No one—not a single legislator, railroad operator, golfer, or farmer—voiced an objection. "Times have changed," an ICC commissioner told Congress, the only congregation of people in the country who had yet to reach consensus on the desperate need for uniform national time legislation. "Railroad time has lost its significance."

Chapter Ten

Lawmakers and Jawbreakers

A committee is a group that keeps minutes and loses hours.
— MILTON BERLE, 1954

$\mathcal{B}$y the early 1960s, no one was in charge of the nation's clocks. Interstate commerce, communication, and travel were as discombobulated as they had been prior to the imposition of Railroad Time in 1883. The short trip from Steubenville, Ohio, to Moundsville, West Virginia, became a symbol of the deteriorating situation. A bus ride down this thirty-five-mile stretch of highway took less than an hour. But along that route, the local time changed seven times. There were thousands of similar cases of horologic schizophrenia in the United States, and the principal cause of the disease was Daylight Saving. After 1955, many cities had followed New York's lead and extended the Daylight period to six months, from the last Sunday in April to the last Sunday in October. But many had not. As a result, bus companies operating between Chicago and Minneapolis had to revise and reprint their schedules five times a year, just to keep up with the seasonal clock changes in

Illinois, Wisconsin, and Minnesota. In Virginia, the schedules for
bus travel within the state had to be reprinted four times over the
course of four months every year.

Despite its reputation for meddling, the federal bureaucracy did
not intervene. Left to their own devices, private enterprise and local
governments—which had repeatedly demanded the right not to alter
their clocks—took to changing the time as often as they changed
their socks, setting off a nationwide frenzy of time tampering that
lasted until 1966. In Indiana, forty-three counties in the Central Time
Zone up and moved themselves into the Eastern Time Zone, without
the approval of the Interstate Commerce Commission (ICC). After
that, state business was conducted and recorded without the benefit
of a common, official time. St. Joseph County, home to the city of
South Bend, initially decided to stay on Central Time. Then, in 1962,
the county suddenly shoved its clocks ahead by an hour, long after
regional timetables had been established. That autumn, busloads of
football fans arrived an hour late for Notre Dame home games.

By 1962, the agricultural state of Iowa boasted twenty-three distinct combinations of dates for starting and ending Daylight Saving.
Apparently, many people in Iowa farming communities had warmed
up to the idea of extended summer evenings since their chickens
and cows had become factory workers who rarely saw the sun. But
in honor of the proud tradition of opposing the clock change, state
legislators saw to it that Iowa did not officially countenance Daylight
Saving. As a result, every summer, local hospitals recorded birth and
death times an hour later than did state record keepers, who were
stuck on Standard Time all year. And if you wanted to get out of
Iowa, you had to time your departure carefully. Motorists driving
west through the 5:00 P.M. rush hour in Council Bluffs, Iowa, found
themselves tied up in the 5:00 P.M. rush hour in Omaha, Nebraska,
one hour later.

Travelers reported similar experiences with double-trouble traffic
across the country. Such inconveniences were the norm in Virginia,

where the mix of unsynchronized local Daylight Saving policies was complicated by the entirely unrelated Daylight Saving schedule in neighboring Washington, D.C.—not to mention the bordering states of Maryland, West Virginia, Kentucky, Tennessee, and North Carolina. After a statewide uniform time bill failed to pass by a single vote, one despondent legislator declared, "We have, I am sure, the most confused State in the Union. . . . [I]t would really take an act of Congress to get the great Southern State of Virginia on one time."

It took a brave individual to invite Congress into the affairs of the Old Dominion; proximity to the nation's capital had made Virginians especially allergic to federal intervention. In fact, Virginians didn't even like clocks telling them what to do. In the nineteenth century, according to the University of Virginia's *Cavalier Daily,* "one of the major pastimes of University gentlemen was to ride up and down the Lawn on their horses and shoot at the Rotunda's clock [because it] represented a measured, mechanized, standard time." This was not a fleeting fad. In 1895, clock shooting was so popular that the University of Virginia installed a bulletproof clock in the Rotunda. *Sic Semper Tyrannis* is the state motto: Thus Always to Tyrants. But in 1963, in the capital city, the editors of Richmond's *News Leader* finally wagged a white flag, conceding, "The establishment of uniform time standards seems to us an entirely reasonable exercise of Federal power."

Even then, the Congress was a reluctant hero. Its one foray into the country's clocks—the 1918 law "To Save Daylight and to Provide Standard Time"—had been rated a disaster. For forty-five years, Congress had shouldered the blame for Daylight Saving, although it had endorsed the plan only briefly—both times at the request of wartime commanders in chief, and both times reluctantly. Congress was also the scapegoat for all the inequities and inconveniences of Standard Time, which had been devised by the railroads and administered for the convenience of commerce without congressional approval.

From the first, federal legislators had not wanted to be in the business of timekeeping or time management. Even as it passed the 1918 legislation, the Congress washed its hands of all oversight and enforcement duties. It granted cities and towns the right to opt out of Daylight Saving, even during the wars. It designated the ICC as arbiter of the time zones. And its Standard Time legislation imposed neither penalties nor fines on communities, states, businesses, or individuals who did not observe Standard Time. As far as Congress was concerned, Americans could use local time, Universal Time, God's time, or even Gittler Time—a method of easing in and out of Daylight Saving "that for three days drove the entire family and all his business associates crazy," according to Gittler's son, Harvey, writing in the *Wall Street Journal.*

> Each day he set his bedroom clock and wristwatch ahead or back fifteen minutes, depending upon the season. That way, he gained or lost only 15 minutes a day. It was a satisfactory arrangement for him, but completely unsatisfactory for everyone else. For three days, he arrived at work 45 minutes, 30 minutes, or 15 minutes early or late. . . . [W]hen someone would ask him what time something would take place, he would always answer, "Your time or my time?" The response was always, "What the devil do you mean?" But he never explained what he meant. It was too complicated for the average person to understand.

By 1963, no federal agency or commission was even attempting to keep track of timekeeping practices in the United States. This must have been especially hard for Congress to understand because, in 1959, it had established a twenty-six-member, bipartisan Advisory Commission on Intergovernmental Relations (ACIR). The ACIR was specifically instructed "to give continuing study to the relationship among local, state, and national levels of government." Four years later, when the Senate finally convened hearings on the feasibility of imposing uniform timekeeping habits on the country, the chairman of the ACIR did not appear. He did send a brief letter to update the senators on his commission's progress. Admittedly, he wrote, the ACIR repeatedly "received suggestions to undertake a study of the intergovernmental implications of time uniformity." However, he added, "It has not done so." Instead of proposing a plan to redress his commission's fundamental failure, and in lieu of an explanation, the ACIR chairman eloquently articulated the basic rules and strategy for the popular bureaucratic game of Hot Potato:

> The ramifications of the issue are so numerous and the interests involved so extensive that the whole matter should be aired in the forum of public hearings. Although authorized by its enabling Act to do so, the [ACIR] has not felt it is equipped to undertake the kind of public hearings the question of time uniformity deserves. In light of the foregoing considerations, we believe that [congressional] hearings are essential to identify the points of agreement and disagreement among the different levels of government concerned. If our staff can be helpful in any way to your staff in this connection, please let us know.

Daylight Saving landed in the hands of Congress in 1963. At the same moment, the ICC was preparing to toss the responsibility for the time zones back to Capitol Hill. When the Senate saw what was coming, it panicked. It dropped all the Uniform Time proposals it had been debating for several years and, instead, proposed to further complicate matters by inventing four new subzones—one in each of the four Standard Time zones. This was even more fantastic than it seemed at first glance. These new subzones were not geographical; they were entirely theoretical. The subzones were imaginary spheres encompassing interstate business and federal agencies, which would be required to adopt uniform dates for Daylight Saving Time, without regard for prevailing local, county, or state practices.

The subzone proposal died on the floor of the Senate. And for almost three years, members of both houses of Congress sat on their hands—plenty of time for the uniformity issue to die a natural death. Two things kept it alive. One was a statement given during the Senate hearings by a former representative from Georgia, Robert Ramspeck. "The widespread time confusion of today could well be compounded by tomorrow," he warned. "Many states have considered or are now considering the establishment of new daylight saving practices, including its possible authorization on a year-round basis." This was a wake-up call. Although technological innovation and shifting commercial fortunes had undone the traditional coalition of Daylight Saving opponents, for millions of Americans, the threat of February breakfasts in the dark was reason enough to support Uniform Time legislation, which would fix the dates for Daylight Saving and limit it to spring and summer months.

But the main reason the time-reform impulse did not die was Ramspeck himself. After his stint in Congress, he had become chairman of the Committee for Time Uniformity, a nonprofit lobby formed by the Transportation Association of America. As the designated spokesman for the nation's transportation, communications, and financial industries, Ramspeck commanded attention. He had also enlisted the cooperation of dozens of federal agencies charged with overseeing these industries. But the real source of Ramspeck's authority was not brute force. It was a fourteen-page report he had commissioned from Thomas Pyne, a retired examiner for the ICC. By 1966, when the House held hearings on Uniform Time, Pyne had completed "A Worldwide Survey of Time Observance," which included a comprehensive study of the habits of Americans. And these habits were much worse than the fearful Congress had worried they might be.

Robert Ramspeck's Committee for Time Uniformity was represented at the 1966 House hearings by its executive director, Robert

Redding. He was a man of few words. "I would not propose to discuss the 1965 pattern of observance other than to say that daylight saving last year was observed in 36 of 50 states." Not only was observance sometimes statewide, sometimes local, and often of uncertain duration, said Redding, but in nonobservant jurisdictions like Tucson, "when daylight saving became effective elsewhere in the country, there were almost 40 schedule changes of the common carriers serving that city, even though it was in a state not observing any daylight time." He mentioned that there were 130 cities in the country with populations of over 100,000; of these cities, 59 did not observe Daylight Saving. Ignoring the management and administrative costs attributable to this complexity, Redding pegged the additional cost of simply printing transportation timetables and broadcast schedules at $5 million a year, most of which was reimbursed via taxpayer-funded subsidies from the Civil Aeronautics Board.

The statistics were compelling, but the anecdotes the Committee for Time Uniformity had turned up were unforgettable. When Yugoslav President Marshal Tito visited the United States, his airport welcome was muffed because his plane landed in a Virginia town that hadn't advanced its clocks with the rest of the state. Pentagon officials flew to Alaska and arrived two hours late for a military conference because no one in Washington, D.C., knew what time it was out there on the Russian border. Alaskans were divvied up into four time zones, but the state only countenanced two zones. A man in Wheaton, Minnesota, said he was opposed to Daylight Saving "because the extra hour of sunlight turned my grass brown." And in St. Paul, someone stumbled onto an eighteen-story office building in which nine floors of city employees did observe, and nine floors of county employees did not observe, Daylight Saving, reflecting an annual division of the Twin Cities.

"It is, of course, enough that the State law sets unique switchover dates for Minnesota on the fourth Sunday in May, the 28th day of May, and the Tuesday after Labor Day, September 6," explained Representative Joseph Karth of Minnesota.

But it also permits [the] local option for border municipalities.... I might say that at one time, St. Paul was on one time, Minneapolis, the sister city, which is only separated by a river, was on another time, and Duluth, Minn., the other major metropolitan area in the State of Minnesota was on Wisconsin Time, to give you an idea of the chaos that reigned. The Minnesota legislature, after futilely considering the complexities of the problem, adjourned.

When the congressional hearings were convened in February 1966, there were seventeen Uniform Time bills languishing in the House of Representatives. America's shameful timekeeping habits had been legendary; now they were matters of fact. The Committee for Time Uniformity had opened up a treasure chest, and it was plundered for thousands of newspaper stories about the anomalies and inanities of American timekeeping. Before the end of March, Uniform Time legislation had passed by a voice vote in the Senate and by a vote of 281 to 91 in the House. President Lyndon Johnson signed the bill into law on 13 April 1966, one year before it took effect. Six months later, he sealed the deal by creating the Department of Transportation, a cabinet-level authority whose jurisdiction included the nation's eight time zones—the four established continental zones and the newly designated Yukon, Alaska-Hawaii, and Bering zones, which formally acknowledged established time practices, as well as the new Atlantic Zone, which included Puerto Rico and the Virgin Islands.

The Uniform Time Act of 1966 established a fixed, six-month period for Daylight Saving Time, from the last Sunday in April to the last Sunday in October. This applied to all fifty states. An individual state could only exempt itself from Daylight Saving by an act of its legislature, and the entire state had to observe a uniform policy throughout the year. For the twelve states whose territory was divided by a time-zone boundary, this requirement of uniformity was perceived as a hardship. Representative Gerald Ford of Michigan repeatedly argued for an amendment that would grant his state the option to use Daylight Saving to coordinate clocks in the Eastern and Central Time zones. But time juggling was precisely what Congress did not want to encourage. Moreover, the reason a big hunk of Michigan was in the Eastern Time Zone was that the state had successfully petitioned the ICC to put it there in 1918. Gerald Ford was advised to try to have that boundary moved again.

The Uniform Time Act was a coup for the persistent proponents of Daylight Saving. During the congressional hearings, representatives of rural districts raised a few objections on behalf of schoolchildren. And Congressman Kenneth Gray of Illinois blamed Daylight Saving for some tragic deaths, "because many people trying to meet the schedules of travel or meetings, find that the time has advanced in another city and not having allowed themselves an extra hour or two, rush unnecessarily. I have heard of instances of loss of life." But there was no serious challenge to the new law. Daylight Saving, long blamed for the collapse of Standard Time in America, had become the national standard for half of every year.

The Uniform Time Act was also a vindication for New York City. The *New York Times* praised lawmakers for finally resolving "the confusion encountered by large metropolitan business concerns," though it hastened to add that the "new legislation will have no effect on the residents of Northeastern states, including New York, for they already observe uniform daylight saving." Along with many newspapers, the *Times* also hailed the 1966 legislation as "the first peacetime move by the Congress to unscramble the confusion that plagues the nation each year." At that moment, there were 190,000 American soldiers in Vietnam. President Johnson had refused to seek a formal declaration of war, perpetuating a spurious debate about what those Americans were doing over there. By 1969, the total troop deployment exceeded half a million, Richard Nixon was in the White House, and he did not seek a formal declaration of war. Neither Congress nor the country ever declared itself. Johnson and Nixon didn't even ask Congress to declare War Time in America.

In 1966, there had been a few skirmishes in individual states about the new Uniform Time law. Hawaii and Arizona legislators acted decisively, and immediately opted out of Daylight Saving. Michigan followed them, but only after holding a statewide referendum, which Daylight supporters lost by fewer than five hundred votes. Alaska, Kentucky, and North Dakota waffled, but eventually adopted Daylight Saving. After that, America's clocks might have entered a new era of relative peace, if it weren't for the state of Indiana.

Hugh Vail, a resident of Indianapolis, was attempting to rally the dispirited rural opposition to Daylight Saving around the country. He didn't succeed, but his wild oratorical flourishes certainly reminded opponents and proponents that there was plenty of life left in the Daylight controversy. The *New York Times* reported on Vail's attempt to scare Iowans back to God's time in 1967.

A child gets up in the morning under daylight time and cries because he has just lost an hour of sleep," Mr. Vail asserted. "A parent has to whip him to get him to go to school. Maybe he has had breakfast and maybe not. He whines all day. When he comes home, his parents give him an aspirin. We are living in a drug age. The schoolchildren are so busted that they have to have drugs. Then when Communism comes along, what are we going to do?

Someone should have given the state of Indiana an aspirin. It had a fever no one could cure. The governor tried to move the entire state into the Central Time Zone in 1967. His petition to the Department of Transportation was followed by almost twenty thousand letters from indignant Hoosiers who objected to the transfer. A call for public comment on the same question in 1969 generated more than a hundred thousand written comments. After dozens of legislative sessions and thousands of suggestions from across the country, Indiana ended up with a time-zone mess so impressive that Congress was compelled to invent a solution. In 1972, citing the unresolved commercial and governmental complications in Indiana and other states with two time zones, Congress amended the Uniform Time Act. In fact, it undermined the principle of uniformity by granting the time-zone-divided states the option to use Daylight Saving Time in none, one, or both of their time zones. This amendment not only helped reignite the national Daylight controversy; it gave Indiana exactly what it needed to make matters worse. Since then, every Indiana legislature and governor has attempted and failed to put an end to the novelty act that passes for a statewide timekeeping policy. The situation remains fluid today. However, at the turn of the twenty-first century, seventy-six Indiana counties were officially in the Eastern Time Zone, and they did not practice Daylight Saving. In addition, six northwestern counties on the Illinois border and five counties (about 150 miles south) on the Indiana border were in the Central Time Zone, and all eleven of these counties practiced Daylight Saving. Furthermore, two counties on the Ohio border and three counties (about 50 miles southwest) on the Kentucky border were in the Eastern Time Zone, and these five counties practiced Daylight Saving.

On 7 November 1973, President Richard Nixon, an outspoken proponent of God's time during the 1960s, delivered a televised address to the nation in which he proposed a comprehensive legislative response to the dramatic international energy crisis: "First," he said, "it would authorize an immediate return to Daylight Saving Time on a year-round basis." He several times compared his plan to the Manhattan Project, and without a hint of irony, he explained exactly what he meant. "Whenever the American people are faced with a clear goal and they are challenged to meet it, we can do extraordinary things."

Nixon had dropped a bomb, but it didn't explode for a few months.

By 1970, most Americans had heard speculation about an impending fuel shortage. The United States, like most industrialized nations, was using much more energy than it was producing. With approximately 6 percent of the world's population, America accounted for 30 percent of the world's annual energy consumption. In October 1973, when the Arab nations of the Organization of Petroleum Exporting Countries (OPEC) responded to American and European support for the nation of Israel by imposing an oil embargo, those rumors were confirmed. The embargo drove up the price of foreign oil by 400 percent in three months. Within a year, the average citizen's annual energy costs rose by five hundred dollars. When you tossed in home and office heat rationing, reduced highway speed limits, and long lines at gasoline pumps, where the price per gallon rose from thirty-five cents to fifty-six cents by the summer of 1974, the inconvenience of year-round Daylight Saving seemed minor to most Americans.

Nixon asked for two years of uninterrupted Daylight Saving. By December, one month after his televised speech, both houses of Congress had signed off on the necessary amendments of the Uniform Time Act, after very little debate and with overwhelming majorities. Congress exempted Hawaii from the two-year clock change, because of the state's nearly equatorial location, and renewed the exemption for Indiana and the eleven other states with two time zones, making that concession a permanent loophole in the Uniform Time Act. In January 1974, the two-year period of Daylight Saving began. It was suspended ten months later. The president's energy plan was in trouble, and so was the president.

In his November 1973 televised speech about the energy crisis, Nixon had also acknowledged "the deplorable Watergate matter. . . . I have even noted that some publications have called on me to resign," he said, adding, "I have no intention whatever of walking away from the job I was elected to do." Nine months later, facing impeachment on three counts, he became the first president in history to resign. Vice President Gerald Ford, the former Michigan congressional representative, pardoned his disgraced predecessor, but he couldn't salvage his Daylight Saving plan. It had blown up during its first month.

It began with a celestial omen. On 8 January 1974, the day after year-round Daylight Saving went into effect, the moon was as near to the earth as it had been in three hundred years. Coastal communities braced for flood tides. But according to the *New York Times,* the biggest disaster in New York City was the rotten metropolitan mood on Monday morning, when the sun didn't rise until 8:20 A.M. A congressman from West Virginia told the *Times* the effect was evident inland, as well: "Most people don't like the idea of getting up in the middle of the night," he said. "It makes them much grouchier until mid-morning." Within a week, school systems in at least five states had delayed opening times by an hour. They were worried about young children who had to negotiate the morning traffic in the dark.

The Edison Electric Institute reported that electric power use for the first week of January Daylight Saving was down by more than 4 percent from the previous year, but most local and regional utility companies estimated that the clock change was responsible for less than 1 percent of the decrease. A week later, there was no apparent saving. Most industry analysts concluded Daylight Saving was a losing proposition. The schools agreed. The superintendent of schools in West Virginia's Mercer County told the *New York Times,* "We use up much more fuel in the coldest part of the day, early morning, to get the schools ready to open. Meanwhile, the lights are blazing and have to be kept on at least through the first period." Her district had not delayed the start of school, because it would have meant "working parents have to leave their youngsters at home unattended when they go off to work." And there was renewed grumbling among coal miners about the hardship of facing a day underground after eating breakfast in the dark. The *Times* detected a widespread "brooding resentment over this latest insult to the intelligence of a people who have experienced so many false pronouncements from their leaders."

Before the end of January, newspapers around the country reported a startling statistic from Florida. Eight schoolchildren had been killed in traffic accidents during the first month of Daylight Saving. A spokesman for the Florida Education Department told the *New York Times* that "six of the deaths were clearly attributable to the fact that children were going off to school in darkness." On the first day of February, a pickup truck hit an eight-year-old boy waiting for a school bus in Atlanta. Georgia's governor, Jimmy Carter, went to the state legislature for a resolution demanding repeal of year-round Daylight Saving. Legislators in California were preparing a similar resolution, according to the *Oakland Post,* since California Highway Patrol records showed "that in the first three weeks of Day-light Saving Time five school-age children have been killed in predawn accidents." Idaho and Oregon sought and won exemptions from wintertime Daylight Saving from the Department of Transportation, and Kentucky had its time-zone boundaries refitted again to counter the effect of the clock change.

In August 1974, the House of Representatives held hearings on the matter. Ohio and South Carolina both reported two school-children killed in morning traffic accidents. A Kentucky congress-man proposed a bill to reduce summertime Daylight to a four-month period "to lead our country out of the present dark-ness." A representative from West Texas testified to 9 A.M. sunrises in his district, which were devastating the harvest and lowering the yields of dairy farmers, one of whom complained, "You can legislate daylight saving time until you are blue in the face, but the dew is going to dry off the field on standard time." The Upper Peninsula of Michigan topped the Texans; in January, folks up there couldn't see by the dawn's early light until 9:30 A.M.

By the end of the first day of congressional hearings, ten states had reported increases in traffic fatalities involving schoolchildren. The Department of Transportation's report to Congress showed a decrease in fatalities for both January and February 1974 compared with the previous year, although it did indicate that more children had died in the early morning hours of January in 1974 than in 1973. This emotionally charged issue defied rational analysis. Estimates for the total number of schoolchildren whose deaths were clearly attributable to the two months of wintertime Daylight Saving in 1974 ranged from 2 to 30. No one on the floor of the House asked, but more than 40,000 Americans had died in motor vehicle accidents that year. Historically, this represents the low end of the range for traffic fatalities; from 1960 through 2000, the annual vehicular death toll varied from 37,000 to 50,000.

Congress pressed the Department of Transportation to provide statistical analyses of the effectiveness of year-round Daylight Saving in the conservation of energy. Despite its repeated assertion that no statistically relevant data could be extracted from such a brief experiment, the Department of Transportation produced a remarkable collection of charts, graphs, and interpretive narrative. The data seemed to indicate no appreciable reduction in gasoline use, a possible increase in the consumption of heating fuels, and a 0.5 to 1.0 percent decrease in electricity demand, most of which was recorded as a saving in coal, the most abundant fossil fuel in the country. Having perused the report, Representative Charles Rose of North Carolina concluded, "The definition of daylight saving time by an old Indian as 'the white man cutting an inch off the bottom of his blanket and sewing it to the top to make it longer' would seem to apply to its savings of energy."

It was evident even before the hearings began that Congress intended to repeal its 1973 legislation, so the Department of Transportation pressed for a compromise, which it won. Year-round Daylight Saving was abandoned, and the nation's clocks were set back to Standard Time on the last Sunday of October in 1974. But instead of waiting to spring ahead until the last Sunday of April in 1975, Americans were instructed to advance their clocks on 23 February. This two-month extension of Daylight Saving was effective for one year only, and its stated purpose was to provide for the study of the effect on fuel use in March and April, which time and resources had not permitted in 1974.

Given the mood of the country, it was unusually bold of Congress to sanction this experiment. Many communities were calling on their representatives to repeal Daylight Saving entirely, even in the summer months. The congressional supporters of the two-month extension were helped enormously by the Department of Transportation's failure to collect any statistics about traffic fatalities attributable to Daylight Saving in March or April 1974. There was no evidence that the safety of schoolchildren would be imperiled. And many congressmen justified their vote by asserting that a 1 percent fuel saving was well worth pursuing. This argument would have been more convincing if the OPEC oil embargo had not been lifted in March 1974.

As an energy-conservation method, Daylight Saving was again a resounding failure. But proponents of extended Daylight Saving in Congress were not really chasing statistics or a few lumps of coal. A new and unlikely coalition of powerful commercial interests had begun to suspect that there was gold in those extended evenings.

The experience of year-round Daylight Saving had managed to enflame passions on both sides of the controversy, and this produced a persistent conflagration that consumed a lot of time on Capitol Hill during the next ten years. Because Americans were again receiving reliable supplies of relatively cheap oil, they seemed to believe the worldwide energy crisis had gone the way of long lines at their neighborhood gas stations. In October 1975, the country's clocks were set back to Standard Time, and most states resumed the Uniform Time habit—six months of Standard Time and six months of Daylight Saving. In 1976, the Senate debated and approved a one-month extension of Daylight Saving. President Jimmy Carter signaled his willingness to sign it, but the House of Representatives demurred. In 1981, the House took up the issue and voted for a two-month extension. President Ronald Reagan gave it the thumbs up, but the bill died in the Senate. In 1983, after another long debate, by a vote of 211 to 199 the House rejected the same Daylight-extension bill it had passed two years earlier.

The 1985 congressional hearings on the topic opened with testimony from Representative Silvio Conte of western Massachusetts, who argued for an eight-month period of Daylight Saving beginning on the first Sunday of March. "It could save the American consumers as much as 100,000 barrels of oil a day," he announced, though he didn't reveal his statistical source. "There are estimates that an expanded daylight saving time could result in 200 fewer traffic fatalities per year," he added, and he didn't stop there. "And also there are statistics that show that street crime would be reduced."

The source of these so-called statistics—indeed, the source of all the numbers quoted and misquoted by proponents of extended Daylight Saving during these hearings—was the Department of Transportation (DOT). By 1985, the DOT seemed to be in favor of extending Daylight Saving. But it was leaning toward a piece of legislation that proposed a nuanced approach to the extension, beginning on the third Sunday of March and extending to the first Sunday of November. This plan had the virtue of redressing a long-standing oddity of the traditional six-month Daylight period.

The summer solstice, the day of the most sunlight, falls on 21 June. Americans had long saved daylight for two months before and four months after the summer solstice, which made no practical sense. The effect of saving daylight in mid-March would be the same as the effect in mid-October.

There was no solar logic for delaying the end of Daylight Saving from late October to the first Sunday in November, however. And a number of the DOT's other numbers did little to bolster the logic of extending Daylight Saving at all. For instance, motor vehicle fatalities in the morning hours had declined after clocks were advanced in April 1979 and 1980, but fatalities had increased in 1981. From the raw data, the DOT had deduced "a net decline in school-age morning fatalities following the change to Daylight Saving time," a small bit of good news that was often repeated without an important caveat: "This limited category of pedestrians and pedalcyclists represent such small numbers that random occurrences in any month of the year can significantly affect the trends."

Several lawmakers leaned heavily on the DOT's startling new statistical evidence about the crime-reducing capacity of Daylight Saving. The presumed affinity of criminals for darkness had long fueled speculation that Daylight Saving would discourage muggers, thieves, and vandals, but statistical information was hard to extract from the complicated social phenomenon of street crime. The DOT had turned up evidence that Daylight Saving had reduced crime by 10 to 13 percent over three years. Fans of these figures did not mention that the numbers were derived from a three-year review of crimes committed in Washington, D.C., without filtering for other contributing factors. But in its reporting of this evidence, the DOT had assured readers it was "impossible to conclude with any confidence that comparable benefits would be found nationwide."

As for fuel saving—the primary justification for extended Daylight Saving in 1974 and 1975—the DOT study of that period "found that a two-month extension of daylight saving to March and April might save one percent of electrical energy, or the equivalent of 100,000 barrels of oil daily . . . [and] any energy savings to be realized from extending daylight saving would be small compared to those resulting from price decontrol." Before the end of the first day of hearings, representatives were confidently predicting an annual fuel saving of 2 percent.

The most confounding statistic provided by the DOT was a monthly average clock time for sunrises throughout the entire country. This seems to have originated as a way of making a very simple point—that advancing clocks in mid-March would deliver sunrise times identical to those in mid-October, which the nation had already accepted. One problem with this argument was that the rural communities in the western reaches of each time zone had repeatedly complained that the late sunrise times in September and October were the worst feature of Daylight Saving. Nonetheless, the DOT went to the remarkable bother of figuring out that "actual clock times of sunrises during the third week in March [with Daylight Saving] would average 7:18 A.M." This calculation was a big hit with advocates of the extension, who used the estimate to prove that their opponents had exaggerated the late sunrise times they would experience with March and April Daylight Saving. However, by adding up thousands of sunrise times in locations across the country and dividing that sum by the number of locations sampled, the DOT had simply achieved a crude approximation of mean time—the sunrise time at the center, or meridian, of each time zone, which had been established for almost one hundred years. Despite the DOT's elaborate math, with Daylight Saving in mid-March, the sun would not rise in Amarillo, Texas, until 8 A.M.

But it was the convenience of commerce, not the demeanor of the ranchers in West Texas, that was on the minds of many lawmakers. Since 1973, eight trade associations had formed a Daylight Saving Time Coalition, and together its members represented $135 billion in annual retail sales. The National Association of Convenience Stores alone represented forty thousand outlets and annual sales of $50 billion. In 1984, *Fortune* magazine had estimated that a seven-week extension of Daylight Saving would yield an additional $30 million just for the Southland Corporation's 7-11 stores. This prediction was based primarily on studies of the purchasing history of the nation's 47 million working women, whose demonstrated habit was to shop and buy more during daylight hours, which most analysts attributed to an enhanced sense of personal safety.

The $22 billion sporting goods industry was looking forward to a $20 million annual boost in the sale of tennis rackets and balls, a 30 percent increase in the number of youth soccer games played, and at least a 4 percent increase in sales of inflatable products. The National Golf Foundation anticipated a $46 million rise in sales of clubs and balls, and an increase in industrywide revenues of $200 million to $400 million. Every hour of additional afternoon daylight was a retail bonanza, and even the West Texas ranchers were invited to hop on the gravy train by the spokesman for the $6 billion barbecue industry, Arthur Seeds. He had prepared the most enthusiastic presentation of the day, a celebration of the tremendous popularity of "the barbecue lifestyle." Seeds told the members of Congress that "consumer involvement since the 1940's has grown from virtually nothing to the current level of over 66 million households." Barbecue, he said, "was definitely good for the nation's livestock and meat industry," not to mention the "35,000 people who work for companies that are totally involved in manufacturing barbecue products." Seeds estimated that "42 hours of additional evening daylight for barbecuing consumers" would result in a 15 percent increase in sales of grills, or $85 million; a 15 percent rise in charcoal briquette sales, or $56 million; and a slightly more modest 13 percent bump in sales of starter fluid, or $15 million—not everyone who used briquettes used fluids. Mr. Seeds had done his homework: "Scientific market surveys show that U.S. consumers enjoy barbecuing outdoors because the food tastes good, it is a pleasant diversion to cook outdoors, it is a change of pace, and it provides an opportunity for informal relaxed activity for the entire family."

And there was more good economic news to come. Garden stores, fast-food restaurants, and hotels and motels were waiting in the wings. Their testimony was sure to be fascinating, but the lawmakers who had orchestrated this extended sales pitch on behalf of extended Daylight Saving had anticipated the need for a human-interest story, something as emotionally compelling as their opposition's collection of newspaper photographs, which featured first-graders shivering on trafficky street corners in pitch darkness. Compared with the fate of schoolchildren, golf balls and charcoal briquettes lacked gravitas.

To address this emotional deficit, the Daylight advocates strategically interrupted the testimony of the trade associations so that Fran Denman Counihan and Mindy Berman could have their say. Counihan was director of public information for the RP Foundation Fighting Blindness. In her opening statement, she told Congress that extended Daylight Saving was a precious gift to people who suffered with night blindness, an "opportunity to impact directly on the quality of life of 400,000 Americans—Americans who are affected by retinitis pigmentosa—RP—and other retinal degenerative diseases." Mindy Berman, a volunteer coordinator for the RP Foundation's Youth Program, described the variety of after-school activities, social opportunities, and simple pleasures Daylight Saving had afforded teenagers with the degenerative disorder. After they read their statements, Ms. Counihan mentioned that Mindy was also one of the young people afflicted by the disease. For a few minutes, Mindy responded to stammeringly polite questions from the members of Congress, and then she asked to be excused. Ms. Counihan explained, "Mindy has to get home before it gets dark."

In December 1985, the House of Representatives voted 240 to 157 to extend Daylight Saving in both the spring and the fall. In the final version of the legislation, the starting date was moved back from the last Sunday in April to the first Sunday in April. This preserved Standard Time throughout the country in March, which satisfied the schoolchildren's lobby. The end of Daylight Saving was extended from the last Sunday in October to the first Sunday in November. As the bill went to the Senate, the Reagan administration signaled its approval, and it intelligently urged Congress to take this opportunity to repeal all the exemptions that had been added to the original Uniform Time Act of 1966 for Indiana and the other bifurcated states.

Of the forty-eight contiguous states, only Arizona and Indiana were still exercising the opt-out option, and their refusal to participate in Daylight Saving was costly to commerce and the public. However, states are reluctant to surrender any rights to the federal government, and Senator Wendell Ford of Kentucky—a time-zone-divided state—had made it clear during the Senate hearings in October 1985 that he had a lot of doubts about extending Daylight Saving to seven months. "At home," he said, "we think six months is a compromise." Ford's argument was not purely parochial. He doubted the retail logic, repeatedly reminding his colleagues that there was no such thing as a free lunch: "If [consumers] buy more from convenience stores, they are buying less from supermarkets," he said. "I think there is an economic tradeoff. Some people get hurt."

The trade-off in the Senate was the preservation of the loophole in Uniform Time; divided states retained the right to opt out of Daylight Saving. In addition, to get the votes for the springtime extension, supporters of the bill had to lop off the one-week autumn extension approved by the House. This was a major blow to the National Candy Brokers & Chocolate Manufacturers Association. The last week in October reliably included Halloween.

As Peter Pantuso, spokesman for the candy makers, prepared to make his opening statement, Senator Ford asked, "Today is Halloween, is it not?" A colleague told him it was. Senator Ford said, "The goblins are here."

> Pantuso: I would like to wish all of you a happy Halloween because it is a very happy and festive season.
>   Senator Ford: Are you going to x-ray all the candy that my grandchildren get?

Pantuso: It should not need to be, Senator. Halloween tampering has really not been a problem. It has been more of a misnomer than it has been a concern.

Senator Ford: You might think that is right, but talk to the parents.

The $6 billion candy industry was hoping to reverse the staggering decline in trick-or-treat business caused by apocryphal stories of candy poisoning, and a heightened concern about child abductions, which had recently been cranked up to a hysteria with public-awareness campaigns featuring photographs of missing children on milk cartons. The candy makers told Congress that one of the most important of its published tips for a safe Halloween was "Go out during daylight hours, if possible." They even left a pumpkin filled with candy on the chair of each member of the hearings committee. Still, they left without their week.

Ronald Reagan signed the extension into law in July 1986. Ever since, Americans have sprung forward on the first Sunday of April and fallen back on the last Sunday of October. That's seven out of twelve months every year, which means that Daylight Saving Time has become our Standard Time.

Chapter Eleven

Millennial Fever

And for this cause God shall send them strong delusion, that they should believe a lie.

—PAUL OF TARSUS, CIRCA 51

$\mathcal{I}$n November 1998, the equatorial nation of Tonga adopted Daylight Saving, effective on the last Sunday of October and ending on the last Sunday of March. This had no measurable effect on energy-consumption patterns in the Friendly Islands, but it meant that clocks there would strike midnight on the last day of 1999 one hour before the clocks in neighboring Pacific Island nations. Tonga wanted to host the premier party of the new millennium. The British Royal Geographic Society was not impressed. In a pronouncement that smacked of postcolonial parochialism, the Brits announced that the millennium would dawn first on New Zealand's Pitt Island, which had been observing Daylight Saving for more than twenty years. This contest was not simply an opportunity to host a lavish party; it was a bonanza of free international advertising for tropical destinations, so Fiji shoved its clocks ahead, too, adopting a four-month period of Daylight Saving, from November through February. But by 1998, it was already too late for Fiji, and for Tonga, too.

In 1995, in an effort to amalgamate his territory—thirty-three islands and atolls scattered on either side of the international date line—the president of the tiny Pacific nation of Kiribati had moved the imaginary international date line, which proved to be as flexible as any other time-zone boundary. This put clocks in Kiribati a full eighty minutes ahead of Tonga's timepieces. According to the *Wall Street Journal*, "the change was made for administrative convenience, not just to cash in on the new millennium," and it had gone unnoticed for several years; most cartographers didn't record the revision until 1998, when it began to look like "an unintentioned bonanza."

A contest inevitably produces losers, and a dose of Daylight Saving wasn't much of a consolation prize. The workday for the residents of these Pacific islands was typically arranged to make use of the cool morning hours, so delaying the time of sunrise was not just confusing; it was counterproductive. And then timekeepers in the rest of the world agreed that the old millennium would not really expire until the last day of the year 2000, which prolonged the tropical Daylight Saving experiment for an extra year. In the meantime, scientists at the U.S. Naval Observatory had pinpointed "where the date line intersects the southernmost latitude at which the sun sets fully before rising again," reported the *Canadian Geographic*. "The first point of land on Earth to see the sun on that momentous morning will be a headland of Antarctica between Dibble Glacier and Victoria Bay, inhabited only by penguins."

Despite apocalyptic prophecies from religious fanatics and secular hysteria about the Y2K programming glitch, the earth and its attendant electronic systems survived the passage into the new millennium. However, a lot of God's creatures were still arguing about God's time. Commercial and political pressure from the United

States and Europe for worldwide standards of uniform timekeeping had converted several Middle Eastern nations, including Lebanon, Egypt, and Syria, to Daylight Saving. Iran had been forced by the shah to set its clocks ahead in 1977, an attempt to modulate electricity demands in Tehran and other cities, where severe electricity-rationing measures had failed to sufficiently reduce demand to prevent regular power failures. Daylight Saving was about as popular as the shah himself, and it was soon deposed, along with him and his pro-Western policies. Keeping time more nearly by the sun seemed to make sense in a nation whose new leaders were Muslim fundamentalists. However, blackouts and brownouts did not go away with the shah. And the traditional Muslim observance was based on a lunar calendar, with each month commencing only after the new moon is seen by an appointed holy man or wise man. The correlation of the sun and clocks was irrelevant. So in 1979, the leader of the revolutionary government, Ayatollah Khomeini, redeemed Daylight Saving simply by mandating it. Thus, the world's premier fundamentalist religious regime became the most reliable Daylight Saving nation in the region.

Elsewhere in the Middle East, the clocks were still up in arms. At its inception in 1948, Israel saved daylight, a measure of defense against air raids from hostile Arab neighbors. But Daylight Saving was soon abandoned in Israel, as Orthodox Jews considered it a threat to faithful observance of the Sabbath. The spring clock change allegedly tempted restaurants, movie theaters, and other commercial enterprises to reopen for business before the sun set—which marked the end of the Sabbath—and this, in turn, allegedly tempted Jews to break the Sabbath. Morning rituals were also complicated by Daylight Saving; later sunrise times often compelled observant Jews to report to work before morning prayers, which are traditionally recited after the sun has risen.

Standard Time stood for God's time in Israel. Then, in 1984, the ruling liberal party conducted a two-year experiment with Daylight

Saving. Energy experts told the *New York Times* that Israel had saved more than $4 million annually. The next spring, on the heels of its successful debut, Daylight Saving was abruptly suspended by Interior Minister Rabbi Yitzhak Peretz, leader of the ultra-Orthodox Shas Party, which had a share in the ruling coalition government—and a commitment to strict religious observance. This sudden policy shift inspired a genuinely original response from fans of both Daylight Saving and secularism. "They demonstrated at 6 A.M. outside the minister's Jerusalem home," reported *The Guardian,* "waking him with a cacophony of cuckoo clocks and alarm clocks."

The battle was on. Israel's erratic Daylight Saving policies became a barometer of the variable power of its secular and Orthodox political factions. In the succeeding years, the clock change was summarily adopted and abandoned with almost no advance warning; Daylight Saving was observed for 127 days, extended to 192 days, modified to 155 days, and proposed as a year-round stimulus to industrial productivity, energy saving, and traffic safety. Predictably, the vitriolic timekeeping debate spilled over into the West Bank. Palestinians took to setting their own dates for Daylight Saving, a political protest that began with the intifada, according to the *Jerusalem Report,* and hardened into "another dividing line in a city that has, formally, been unified for more than thirty years."

And then the neighboring nation of Jordan adopted Daylight Saving. When an intrepid reporter for the *Financial Times* attempted to untangle the implications for timekeeping in September 1999, he effectively previewed the diplomatic chaos of the twenty-first century:

> In Palestinian areas of the West Bank, time will be ahead of Israel; the clocks in the Jewish settlements there will be on Israeli time. Anyone continuing to Jordan after a stopover in the PA [Palestinian Authority] controlled territory will revert to Israeli time at the border. . . . All the land border terminals on the Israeli and Jordanian

sides will operate according to Israeli time, even though Jordan is one hour ahead of Israel. Once beyond the Jordanian terminal, time goes forward an hour. To further complicate matters, anyone planning separate meetings with the PA and Jordanian officials in the coming weeks should watch the clock. Jordan intends to retain Daylight Saving.

No place on earth was safe. Daylight Saving was in the air above Africa and Asia, and since 1980, the pattern on both continents had resembled the approach-avoidance strategy of the southern and western United States after World War II. Short-term Daylight experiments were followed by long periods of attachment to Standard Time in Pakistan, Indonesia, and South Korea. In South Africa and India, persistent commercial lobbying efforts have recently succeeded in pushing more than a billion people to the precipice, and if they do spring forward, a billion Chinese might be inspired to take the leap with them.

It wouldn't be the first time. In 1986, having collapsed all four of its time zones into one, the Beijing government unexpectedly launched a five-year program of Daylight Saving, based strictly on Beijing Time. For Chinese in the western provinces, this arrangement was roughly equivalent to living in Los Angeles according to Daylight Saving Time in Washington, D.C. Although a few European nations had briefly experimented with double Daylight Saving, even the British had not attempted to quadruple it. Any saving that was realized in Beijing had to compensate for the costs to outlying industrial and agricultural centers, where clocks lagged more than four hours behind apparent solar time. The sun often rose after noon in China's western provinces, and it did not set until after midnight. And there were no protests reported when the government instructed all clocks to take a great leap back to Chinese Standard Time in 1992—which is Beijing Time all the time.

Still, it would be a mistake to assume that China will be able to resist another outbreak of fast time. Contact with Daylight Saving has never served as an inoculation. It's a persistent virus of an idea that thrives on rejection, as it has in Japan.

By the end of the twentieth century, Daylight Saving was no more appealing to the Japanese than it was when it was foisted upon them by occupation forces after World War II. The faltering Japanese economy, however, which was dependent on trade with Europe and the United States, was in need of stimulation. After more than fifty countries endorsed the 1997 Kyoto Protocol, a trade-based incentive plan for reducing greenhouse gases in industrialized nations, the nation that had hosted the negotiations could no longer afford to ignore the accompanying recommendation of Daylight Saving. In 2003, the Japanese conducted a very tentative Daylight experiment in the Shiga prefecture. Most citizens ignored the voluntary program, which asked government offices to take the lead by "allowing employees to come to work between 30 minutes and one hour earlier if they want," according to *Mainichi Shimbun*. Only 50 percent of Shiga's government workers initially signed up to participate, and only a quarter of these volunteers actually turned up for work an hour early on the first day of the eight-week experiment. Opponents immediately declared it a failure and predicted that private corporations would never support Daylight Saving. They urged the government to revise its target date of 2008 for nationwide adoption. But Shiga's governor shrugged off the discouraging initial results. "If things go well," he told *Mainichi*, "I would like to see this debated nationwide." It was not apparent to everyone, but things were already going well. Although the Japanese had become famous for their rigorous work habits and their willingness to devote long hours to company business, many of Shiga's experimental Daylighters found new uses for their extended evenings. Kenichi Ozawa told *Mainichi* he spent the extra hour of evening light taking a walk with his family. And many other Japanese have taken a shine to extended evenings. Before World War II, there were twenty-three golf courses in Japan, according to the National Golf Foundation; by 2003, there were more than three thousand.

European uniformity on Daylight Saving was achieved largely through the efforts of the Common Market and, later, the European Union. By the beginning of the twenty-first century, Italy, Turkey, Bosnia, Poland, Latvia, Sweden, Iceland, and most of their neighboring nations had adopted a uniform seven-month period of Daylight Saving, which begins on the last Sunday of March.

France resisted—noisily and ineffectively. The French refused to adopt Daylight Saving when their neighbors did at the onset of the 1973–1974 OPEC oil embargo, so by 1976, the worsening energy crisis in France forced the desperate government to impose not one but two hours of Daylight Saving, doubling public outrage. Editorialists and politicians ridiculed the government's reports of projected and real fuel savings, and credulously repeated statistics about the rising incidence of fatigue, nervous exhaustion, and absenteeism throughout the nation. For twenty years, the French pursued a policy of resistance, adoption, and denunciation. In 1985, French environmentalists told a reporter for United Press International that "more sunshine during peak traffic hours produces more ultraviolet rays to break down exhaust fumes into products that cause acid rain." This analysis not only was singular to France but also failed to account for the implied inverse effect of reduced sunlight during morning rush hours. A member of the French Parliament told the same reporter that Daylight Saving upset farmers, "who are still in the field when it's time to watch evening television." Nonetheless, France sprang forward. In 1996, however, Prime Minister Alain Juppé, a staunch conservative, put an end to the madness. He told *U.S. News and World Report* that the French republic would permanently abandon Daylight Saving Time in 1997 because "it is less and less understood by our fellow citizens and is of no economic interest." Instead, his fickle fellow citizens voted him out of office in 1997. In 2004, Juppé was convicted of illegally serving the economic interests of his political allies with public funds. Daylight Saving survived him.

As the originators of modern Daylight Saving, the British were not content to sit idly by at the end of the century while the rest of the world meddled and fussed with their invention. Moreover, Britain's role in timekeeping had suffered a few embarrassing setbacks since World War II. In 1946, light and air pollution from nearby London forced the removal of the Royal Observatory from its storied home in Greenwich to a distant castle in Sussex. And in the 1960s, with the advent of Atomic Time, a more precise statistical timescale supplanted the relatively crude calculus that yielded Greenwich Mean Time. Composed of data from cesium clocks around the world, International Atomic Time (TAI) was computed across the English Channel at the Bureau International de l'Heure in Paris. Of course, daily life in most countries was not governed by Atomic Time, and the British did have a hand in Coordinated Universal Time (UTC)—which tempered Atomic Time with the actual behavior of the earth relative to the sun. However, the contributions of the Royal Observatory were subject to confirmation from several satellites hovering high above.

The British did conduct a memorable three-year experiment with Daylight Saving. All clocks in the kingdom ran one hour faster than normal from 1968 to 1971. This yielded a trove of new data, and a tremendous outcry from residents of Scotland, whose northerly location was already famous for its dark winter mornings and its almost endless summer evenings. The Scots were told to look north and count their blessings. Swedish cities north of the Arctic Circle observed Daylight Saving with their Scandinavian neighbors, including Utsjoki, where the sun rose in mid-May at around 1:00 A.M. and did not set for more than two months.

The data from the three-year British experiment were analyzed in 1988 and again in 1993 by the Policy Studies Institute of London. Along with the previously established benefits to commerce, industry, and public health, Daylight Saving came out a clear winner in the almost universal controversy about the fate of schoolchildren. Although early-morning fatalities involving school-age children had increased with wintertime Daylight Saving, the concomitant reduction in afternoon and evening fatalities among the school-age population was far greater. The 1993 report attributed to Daylight Saving an annual saving of 140 young lives, a total saving of 600 lives across all ages, and an attendant saving of £200 million to the society—with one caveat. This analysis was not simply counting on year-round Daylight Saving; it was counting on an implausible policy of year-round plus summertime Daylight Saving, which it referred to by the acronym SDST, presumably to avoid invoking the plan's implausible common name: Single-Double Summer Time.

In effect, this experiment was an elaborate scheme to move Great Britain into a new time zone, the time zone occupied by most European Union member nations—one hour east of Britain's prime residence in the time zone of the prime meridian. It would have been much easier to say that SDST was French time, though this would not have made it easier to sell.

Not that the British public was buying. Stockbrokers and bankers stood to lose a precious hour of arbitrage with the exchanges in New York City. Farmers would be rewarded with an extra hour of morning dew. And clocks in Greenwich would never correspond to their appointed Greenwich Mean Time. Plus, the British public had just bought the £750 million Millennium Dome, a government-sponsored tourist attraction built at public expense below the site of the old Royal Observatory, and the dome proved so unpopular that it was shuttered and offered for sale before the old millennium had expired.

As the new millennium approached, it was not clear if the sun ever set on the British empire. A research laboratory in Antarctica, a few patches of coral in the Pacific, and a fatuous war with Argentina for sovereignty over the Falkland Islands kept the cliché alive. Perhaps it was more gratifying for the residents of Buckingham Palace to see that Daylight Saving was well established in its biggest former colonies, where the practice continued to wreak havoc. Most Australians in the nation's three time zones observed Daylight Saving from the last Sunday in October to the last Sunday in March, though Tasmanians complicated things by saving daylight from the beginning of October of every year. Meanwhile, residents of New South Wales had turned their clocks ahead two months before everyone else in August 2000 to suit the schedules of the corporations broadcasting the Sydney Olympics, and rural Queensland hadn't bothered about Daylight Saving since the war. Queensland's elected representative, Christine Scott, told the *Northern Miner,* "We don't want it, we don't need it, and we regard it as a time-wasting exercise." Despite pressure from shop owners and bankers bothered by the province's provincial attitude, Scott predicted that her supporters "in the bush" would not cave in. "Most of us, including our hard-pressed primary producers, are already working from *can see* to *can't see,"* she explained, "and there aren't enough hours in the day as it is."

The Australian situation, and the country's long and contentious progress toward a uniform national policy, were mirrored in the Northern Hemisphere by the Canadian experience. By 2000, Canada and the United States had a uniform period of Daylight Saving that was just one week shorter than the European period, and most Canadians in the five continental time zones saved daylight from early April until the end of October. Saskatchewan was a vast exception to the rule. And it was always hard to predict how Newfoundlanders would complicate their peculiar zone time, which was 30 minutes ahead of North America's Atlantic Time. They had experimented with 30, 60, and 120 minutes of Daylight Saving. "Doesn't poor old Newfoundland suffer enough from jokes about it?" wondered a reader of *Maclean's* when the province shoved its clocks out of sync with the rest of the country for the umpteenth time. "One can almost picture the guy with the doomsday sign pacing the street, 'The world ends at noon; 3:15 in Newfoundland.'"

Conformity with the United States was precisely why most Mexicans did not want to adopt Daylight Saving. For seventy years, Mexico had been unmoved by the seasonal oscillations north of the border. But in 1988, the *New York Times* reported on a regional experiment in Mexico's northeastern states, where merchants "had long lobbied for moving clocks ahead so that they could compete with rivals across the [Rio Grande], who could open an hour before shopowners here because Texas is on daylight time." The trial period won local approval, and in 1996 Daylight Saving was nationalized—theoretically.

Several southern Mexican states immediately mounted a legal challenge to the federal government's right to dictate regional social policy. The federal government countered with a claim that it was saving 1 billion kilowatts of electricity. The Associated Press reported that residents of Sonora were demanding an exemption "because their northern state borders Arizona, which does not observe daylight-saving time in the United States." Newspapers from Nuevo Laredo to New York chronicled allergic reactions to the clock change; the complaints ranged from chronic drowsiness to clinical depression—and persistent, almost paranoid speculation that the Clinton administration had made Daylight Saving mandatory in Mexico while negotiating the North American Free Trade Agreement. To prove that it was not toeing the American line, the Mexican government abruptly foreshortened the period of Daylight Saving.

Nothing allayed the lingering suspicion that the White House wanted to control clocks in all of the Americas—least of all President Clinton's first visit to Brazil in the fall of 1997. Clinton was touring South America to promote his expansive idea of Pan-American free trade, and many newspapers in the United States and Canada detected a note of old-fashioned Yankee imperialism. But "no one was prepared," reported the *Washington Times,* "for the demand that Brazil's 160 million people suspend daylight savings [sic] time that day to allow the president another hour to prepare for his evening schedule." The White House denied this report, but it could not deny a headline the *Ottawa Citizen* reprinted from *Veja,* a weekly Brazilian magazine: "The Arrogance of Empire." And the *Citizen* story did not stop there.

> U.S. demands that Brazil should prepare for President Bill Clinton's arrival yesterday by putting back its clocks, shutting down railway service and felling trees that might conceal snipers ensured a peppery welcome for the "arrogant great Gringo." . . . Even President Henrique Cardoso showed a flash of irritation after hearing that the White House wanted to change the time set for a state dinner at his palace. "Who decides about what time I have dinner in my palace?" he asked rhetorically. "That's me."

The Brazilian government did not buy Clinton's free-trade package, and it didn't tinker with Daylight Saving. Throughout the final years of the twentieth century, Brazil annually claimed an impressive energy saving of more than 1 to 3 percent and critical peak-load reductions of more than 5 percent. By 2000, Chile and Paraguay had also permanently adopted the seasonal clock change, and in 1999, Argentina's national legislature approved Daylight Saving for the summer of 2000. Three months before Buenos Aires sprang ahead, however, someone in the government detected distant thunder—presumably, a stampede of protest on the pampas, home to the nation's celebrated beef industry. President Fernando de la Rua's economic advisers produced a new analysis of Daylight Saving, which indicated that Argentines would turn on their lights in record numbers every morning and increase energy consumption by 10 to 15 percent. The president canceled Daylight Saving, and his political future. In 2000, Argentina sped downhill in the darkness, and before its economy finally crashed, the nation had suffered through the most sustained and debilitating energy crisis in its history. Most Argentines have since taken their clocks in hand every spring, hoping to squeeze out an hour's worth of kilowatts.

In the United States, the Uniform Time Act of 1966 had imposed synchronicity on most clocks, but it had not induced uniformity of opinion about the effect of Daylight Saving on energy consumption. Indeed, Daylight's most ardent supporters were merchants and manufacturers, who were convinced that Daylight Saving stimulated consumption. President George Herbert Bush gave this controversy a patriotic spin. "Sunday, October 29, 1989, is the date on which the Nation will return to Standard Time," he reminded Americans two days before the autumn clock change. It was the first time he showed an interest in Daylight Saving. "We may use this adjustment of the clocks as a reminder to perform other simple actions—actions that can save lives by helping to make our homes safe from accidental fire. . . . In particular, we can also take a few minutes to test our home smoke detectors, clean them, and change their batteries."

Most Americans have never actually celebrated "Fire Safety at Home—Change Your Clock and Change Your Battery Day," but millions have observed it every year. Not Michael Brown of Pennsylvania, however. He wasn't lacking in equipment. "I have three types of detectors powered by nine-volt alkaline batteries," he told the *New York Times* in 1995. "In all three types a fresh alkaline battery remains effective for more than two and a half years, as measured by the built-in tester on the Duracell packages. This has astonishing implications for the amount of hazardous waste generated."

Everything associated with Daylight Saving has always involved a trade-off. Although most Americans had never thought about the environmental implications of Change Your Battery Day, a few had carefully considered its astonishing commercial implications. In 1989, the manufacturers of Eveready batteries funded a "public education campaign," which coincided with President Bush's proclamation and featured endorsements from the International Association of Fire Chiefs and the National Burn Association. "The campaign generated 1.5 million media impressions with an advertising equivalency of $20.9 million," reported *Ad Week:*

> The message permeated every layer of print and broadcast media, including front and op-ed pages in many publications. Highlights included USA Today, CNN Headline News, Good Morning America, The Today Show, Larry King Live, and Regis and Kathy Lee.... Eveready credits the campaign with ending a six-year declining trend in brand sales, showing marked increases in October, when the program was held, and sometimes doubling or tripling sales to major chain accounts.

Whenever Americans turned ahead their clocks, somebody turned a profit. By the end of the twentieth century, no one had to lift a hand. Computers, quartz clocks, automated payroll systems, VCRs, DVD recorders, security systems, and most other electronic devices were taught how to perform the spring and fall clock change automatically. This saved time and money—unless you were stuck on a train.

At 2 A.M. on the last Sunday of October, Amtrak conductors stepped on the brakes. While most Americans fell back onto Standard Time and enjoyed an extra hour of sleep, the patrons of the nation's federally subsidized passenger rail system were halted in the middle of their journeys for one hour. This was a long-standing tradition on America's railroad tracks. It guaranteed that trains would not reach their destinations before their scheduled arrival time—though Amtrak still hadn't invented a system to guarantee that its trains wouldn't be late. Indeed, at least once a year, late arrival was guaranteed. According to company policy, "on the first Sunday of April, when most communities set clocks ahead one hour, Amtrak trains will become one hour late. We will attempt to make up this time."

Churchgoers had the same problem; they continued to turn up late for services on the first Sunday of April, despite annual reminders in parish bulletins. The Reverend Robert Sherman of St. Jerome Catholic Church told the *St. Petersburg Times* the impact of Daylight Saving on attendance was most dramatic when the spring changeover coincided with Easter sunrise services. He was sympathetic to the oversleepers, but there was one thing Father Sherman couldn't understand. "How come they never seem to arrive an hour early when Daylight Saving ends in the fall?"

And then all hell broke loose. As the millennium approached, legislators in Massachusetts, Louisiana, Nevada, and California introduced bills calling for year-round Daylight Saving. The Uniform Time Act prevented the states from altering the dates of adoption for Daylight Saving on their own, but Representative Brad Sherman of California submitted a bill to Congress calling for reform of the Uniform Time Act. His immediate goal was more Daylight Saving in California, where the skyrocketing price of electricity had not decreased commercial or residential demand. The outdated power grid responded with rolling blackouts and brownouts in major metropolitan areas. And the federal government was investigating fraudulent accounting practices at Enron Corporation, America's famously profitable and inexplicably bankrupt energy-trading firm, a major force in California's energy sector.

Representative Sherman favored the idea of double Daylight Saving in California, but his proposed legislation actually gave states on the West Coast the right to modify the period and degree of Daylight Saving as they pleased. "The plan is one small part of Texas Rep. Joe Barton's Electricity Emergency Relief Act," reported the *Houston Chronicle* in May 2001. "If it becomes law, California, Nevada, Oregon, and Washington will be able to shift hours of the day to match the schedules of most of their citizens."

This was perceived as a threat to Uniform Time, as other states would surely demand the same privilege. James Benfield, a private energy consultant, told the *Houston Chronicle*, "They can do it, but they'll regret it. They will end up with a patchwork of time zones." One proposed strategy for preserving uniformity under the new law was to erase the boundary between the Rocky Mountain Time and Pacific Time zones. This merger would effectively produce year-round Daylight Saving on the West Coast, which could be doubled every summer—Single-Double Summer Time. If it caught on, the clocks in San Francisco and Seattle would run one hour ahead of clocks in Arizona every summer, and just one hour behind most clocks in Indiana.

The *Jewish Exponent* asked its readers to imagine a scenario in which the Sabbath did not officially end until after 9 P.M.: "Imagine the growling tummies and restless children." This prompted a call to California, and Representative Sherman responded directly to this and all other special-interest bellyaching with apocalyptic rhetoric. "We've got an immediate crisis here," he told the *Exponent*. "People are going to die." There had been reports of heat-related deaths in California's cities, and the state was developing emergency plans to assist the elderly and the ill during the upcoming summer months. But Sherman's righteousness was not a substitute for being right. The optimistic 1993 British study of Single-Double Summer Time had projected a "likely" reduction in lighting costs, a small increase in heating costs for commercial buildings, and a 3 percent reduction in peak-load demands for electricity, though "no figures are available on the scale of those savings."

Sherman confidently predicted that double Daylight Saving would reduce total energy consumption on the West Coast by an additional 1 percent, though there were no known American data about a second hour of Daylight Saving. And no one had absolutely established an actual saving with even one hour of Daylight. Sherman also mentioned that his plan might also reduce traffic fatalities and violent crime. This betrayed his source; he was citing statistics from the inconclusive analyses conducted by the Department of Transportation twenty-five years earlier.

In May 2001, Congress convened hearings on the energy conservation potential of Extended and Double Daylight Saving Time. No one doubted the gravity of the nation's energy woes. No one could quite believe that the Daylight Saving controversy was back on the national agenda. Everyone knew it wasn't going away anytime soon, because no one could yet determine whether Daylight Saving saved energy. California Congresswoman Lynn Woolsey, the ranking member of the Subcommittee on Energy of the House Committee on Science, did her best. At one point in the day, she turned her full attention to Linda Lawson, the acting deputy assistant secretary for transportation policy:

> Woolsey: How are we going to find out how much energy this could save? Because that is what it has got to be based on if we are going to, you know, argue the benefits, we have got to know what those benefits are. And your data, Ms Lawson, is how old?
>
> Lawson: I would say it is very old and it was also for a very limited time. We only looked at four transitional dates. I would suggest that my colleagues at the Department of Energy might be able to provide more information on this.
>
> Woolsey: Okay. Thank you.

The other principal witness was James Benfield, the private energy consultant who had warned the readers of the *Houston Chronicle* about the importance of preserving Uniform Time. Ben-

field had been here before, and his opening statement on the floor
of the House of Representatives was a trip down memory lane. "In
1984, I founded the Daylight Saving Time Coalition [the golf, barbecue, and candy lobby], which led the successful effort to move the
starting date of Daylight Saving to the beginning of April. I am
speaking today as a private individual. During our two-year campaign, we never used the argument that more Daylight Saving Time
would save energy." This was strictly true, but the spring extension
of Daylight Saving he had secured for his retail clients in 1985 would
not have won congressional approval without the attendant expectations for reductions in crime, traffic fatalities, and, most importantly,
energy consumption.

Benfield launched into a long review of the highlights of Daylight
Saving in the United States. His opening statement did not throw
any light on the pertinent question of energy. It did illuminate the
terms of the Daylight Saving debate for the new millennium. The
transportation, communication, and retail industries wanted to preserve Uniform Time, which served their economies. This might
involve the occasional trade-off with the health and well-being of
some of their loyal consumers. The states were agitating for more
control over their increasingly disparate local and regional power-
management issues. This might involve the occasional trade-off with
the health and well-being of some of their loyal citizens. By May
2001, Daylight Saving was the cornerstone of both sides of the controversy. The perennially divided Congress was stuck in between.

"In summary," concluded Benfield, "year-round Daylight Saving
Time should not be observed unless energy savings can be clearly
proven to the public."

Representative Woolsey had the floor. She spoke directly to Benfield, but she was speaking for all Americans when she said, "I am
more confused than I was when we started."

Acknowledgments and Sources

My initial attempts to answer fundamental questions about Daylight Saving Time by consulting the obvious sources quickly degenerated into a multiple-choice test. There were many explanations, most of them contradictory. The source of most of this confusion was Congress. Discord, of course, is the mark of a truly democratic forum. If you give everyone a chance to speak, by the end of the day, almost everything will have been said. I did not immediately see the virtue in this.

With the invaluable assistance of the staff in Government Documents at Harvard University's Lamont Library, I located and read transcripts of many of the legislative sessions and committee meetings that compose the century-long Daylight Saving debate on Capitol Hill. I first encountered most of the substantive material for this book in the texts of the congressional hearings—oral and written testimony given to the U.S. Senate and the House of Representatives, as well as letters, petitions, reports, and studies submitted by legislators, individual citizens, private interest groups, public agencies, and commercial institutions. Everything was there except a logical explanation for Daylight Saving Time.

After my initial, confounding encounter with Congress, Marcia McClintock Folsom, a great friend and a generous colleague, alerted me to Michael O'Malley's compelling and cogent social history of the mechanization of time in the United States through 1920: *Keeping Watch: A History of American Time* (New York: Viking, 1990). O'Malley's analysis of the opportunism that attended the initial Daylight Saving legislation in the United States illuminated the public record for me. Moreover, O'Malley's inspired use of eclectic sources encouraged me to pay attention to anomalies and absurdities in general, and to the specific influence of the retail and leisure industries as they emerged and changed throughout the century.

Three cities figured prominently in every stage of this history— London, New York, and Washington, D.C. Fortunately for me, each is represented by a distinguished newspaper that survived the twentieth century—no mean feat. I leaned heavily on the work of reporters and editors at the London *Times,* the *New York Times,* and the *Washington Post* to characterize the significance of Daylight Saving in the public imagination and to track its effect on the daily lives of Americans and other people around the world. I am deeply grateful to the working writers at these and other newspapers and periodicals. These journalists not only chronicled the peculiar details of the story but perennially elicited responses from readers in the form of editorials and letters that document passionate allegiances and profound allergies to Daylight Saving—responses that would otherwise have remained private. The staff at the Tufts University Computing and Communications Service provided me with technical assistance and occasionally performed an emergency intervention that made electronic access to much of this information a reality.

A compendium of the sources I used, keyed to phrases in the text, follows this note. In lieu of footnotes, I have identified my principal sources in the text. I hope this choice to alert readers to contemporary reporting in context re-creates my own experience of discovering the proportions of the Daylight Saving debate in the United States. The contradictions and confusion occasioned by authoritative sources throughout the century are not ancillary to this story; contrariety is the beating heart of this endless controversy.

In the course of my research, I read and explored hundreds of Web sites and weblogs, where facts, fallacies, and conspiracy theories are served up in nearly equal proportions. Two Web sites inspired me. Yugo Nakamura's *Industrious 2001* (www.lares.dti.ne.jp/~yugo/storage/monocrafts_ver3/03/index) and Parker Croft's *Time for One World* (parkercroft.com) are both arresting visual representations of the problem of recorded time.

Michelle Blake listened to every thought I had about this book and responded with her remarkable combination of intelligence and kindness, and when I finally had a manuscript, she read it and improved every page. Mary Ann Matthews was encouraging and sympathetic in just the right proportions. She read many drafts of this book, and every one of her astute comments and questions made it better. I am indebted to Jeanne Heifetz, Alexandra Zapruder, Jessica Kane, James Lecesne, Sharon Morrison, John Harrington, Marcia Fields, Monica Klein-Samanez, Phil Bennett, and Peter Kassel for their sustained and sustaining enthusiasm and their many useful suggestions.

Three people merit special mention. My editor, Jack Shoemaker, responded to my initial, uninformed idea for this book as if it were a serious proposal and gave me the good advice he always gives me, which I often forget for months at a time: Write it. Thanks to his repeated advice, I did. My agent, Jonathan Matson, believed in this book and its writer even when the writer had his doubts. And Peter Bryant was, as ever, my first and best reader and my constant companion. He makes time for me whenever I need it, which is the Daylight Saving plan I heartily endorse.

ABBREVIATIONS

Newspapers

LT	London *Times*
NYT	*New York Times*
WP	*Washington Post*

Congressional Hearings

HH 1919   House Committee on Interstate and Foreign Commerce, *Repeal of Section Three of the Daylight Saving Act,* parts 1, 2, and 3, 2–3 June 1919 (Washington: Government Printing Office, 1919).

HH 1966   House Committee on Interstate and Foreign Commerce, *Uniform Time,* 2 February 1966 (serial no. 89-28) (Washington: Government Printing Office, 1966).

HH 1974   House Committee on Interstate and Foreign Commerce, Subcommittee on Commerce and Finance, *Time Amendment: 1974,* 12 August 1974 (serial no. 93-89) (Washington: Government Printing Office, 1974).

HH 1985   House Committee on Energy and Commerce, Subcommittee on Energy Conservation and Power, *Daylight Saving Time,* 24 April 1985 (serial no. 99-4) (Washington: Government Printing Office, 1985).

HH 2001   House Committee on Science, Subcommittee on Energy, *Energy Conservation Potential of Extended and Double Daylight Saving Time,* 24 May 2001 (serial no. 107-30) (Washington: Government Printing Office, 2001).

SH 1963   Senate Committee on Commerce, *Uniform Time Legislation,* 29 April 1963 (Washington: Government Printing Office, 1963).

SH 1973   Senate Committee on Commerce, *Daylight Saving Time*, 9 and 12 November 1973 (serial no. 93-49) (Washington: Government Printing Office, 1974).

SH 1985   Senate Committee on Commerce, Science, and Transportation, Subcommittee on Science, Technology, and Space, *Daylight Savings* [sic] *Extension Act of 1985*, 31 October 1985 (serial no. 99-380) (Washington: Government Printing Office, 1986).

CHAPTER ONE: THE INFINITE HOUR

1   *House of Representatives voted 252 to 40*   For congressional vote tallies, I relied principally on reporting in *NYT* and *WP*.

2   *"The new daylight saving system"*   *NYT*, 16 March 1918, 1.

2   *"Nobody is opposed"*   *NYT*, 5 March 1918, 10.

2   *"has indorsed*   *Springfield (Mass.) Republican,"* in *Current Opinion* 62 (March 1917): 161.

3   *1784 letter*   Benjamin Franklin, letter to *Journal of Paris*, 1784, in webexhibits.org/daylightsaving/franklin3.html.

3   *"I observ'd"*   Benjamin Franklin, *The Autobiography*, in *Benjamin Franklin: Writings*, ed. J. A. Leo Lemay (New York: Library of America, 1987).

4   *"they were repulsed"*   *LT*, 25 May 1909, 5.

4   *"Light is one"*   This and all citations to William Willett appear in William Willett, *The Waste of Daylight* (London: 1907), self-published pamphlet.

5   *"little less than"*   *NYT*, 3 July 1909, 6.

5   *Royal Astronomer*   *Notes and Records of the Royal Society of London* 8, no. 2 (April 1951): 131–148.

6   *"German Summer"*   *LT*, 6 May 1916, 5.

6   *Frankfurt's daily*   *LT*, 13 April 1916, 7.

6   *"Millions of dollars"*   All quotations attributed to the president of the AAAS appear in *Current Opinion* 62 (February 1917): 141.

7   *$110 million*   *NYT*, 11 November 1918, 6.

7   *"the only reform"*   *NYT*, 5 March 1918, 10.

7   *"General efficiency"*   Boston Chamber of Commerce, "An Hour of

Light for an Hour of Night," report of the Special Committee on Daylight Saving Plan, in *Current Affairs* supplement (19 March 1917), 3–5.

8	*"it upsets all"* NYT, 11 June 1919, letter, 14.

8	*"It prevents"* Ibid.

9	*"light is a physical"* Current Opinion 62 (February 1917): 141.

9	*"She opposed it"* NYT, 4 October 1919, 3.

9	*"Our last hour"* Current Opinion 62 (February 1917): 141.

9	*"It robs"* NYT, 11 June 1919, letter, 14.

9	*"Daylight saving was brought"* Irving Fisher, "Consideration of the Proposal to Stabilize the Unit of Money," *American Economic Review* 9, no. 2 (June 1919): 256–262.

9	*"Rather than change"* Ralph Demos, "Legal Fictions," *International Journal of Ethics* 34, no. 1 (October 1923): 37–58.

10	*"a man cheating"* NYT, 13 March 1926, letter, 22.

10	*"I'm fooled"* Woman Citizen, 3 June 1922, 6.

10	*"Changing the clock"* NYT, 4 October 1919, 3.

11	*"A reliable clock"* NYT, 31 March 1918, advertisement, 50.

11	*"The French call"* NYT, 5 June 1932, X7.

11	*"Daylight Saving means an extra"* NYT, 19 March 1918, advertisement, 18.

11	*"sixty minutes"* NYT, 7 January 1917, S1.

11	*"law was intended"* NYT, 2 April 1918, 15.

12	*"lobbying organization"* Michael O'Malley, *Keeping Watch: A History of American Time* (New York: Viking, 1990), 291–292.

13	*"our society's"* Margaret Mead, "Popular Opinion Mechanisms Among Primitive Peoples," *Public Opinion Quarterly* 1, no. 3 (June 1937): 5.

13	*"100 million"* The Nation, 10 May 1965, 491.

13	*"one of the big issues"* NYT, 25 September 1966, 51.

14	*(apparently) noon* Richard Kujawa, "Standard Time," Web page, at http://academics.smcvt.edu/geography/standard.htm, adapted from Carlton J. Corliss, *The Day of Two Noons* (Santa Fe: Association of American Railroads, 1952), and Fred M. Shelley and Audrey E. Clarke, *Human and Cultural Geography* (Dubuque: William C. Brown, 1994).

15	*"The Pennsylvania Railroad"* Carsten Möller, "The Day of Two Noons," Web page, at www.Fremo.org/betrieb/timezone.htm, adapted from Carlton J. Corliss, *The Day of Two Noons* (Santa Fe: Association of American Railroads, 1952).

17   *"The latest train"* NYT, 30 March 1918, 13.

CHAPTER TWO: THE FARMER IN THE DEW

19   *"that fateful day"* NYT, 24 October 1995, letter, A26.

20   *"because of a stupid"* San Francisco Chronicle, 22 November 1993, letter, A30.

20   *"Why do we have to"* "Stuii," weblog comments, at www.aber.org.uk, accessed February 2004.

20   Ask a Scientist   Argonne National Laboratory, "Ask a Scientist, General Science Archive" Web page, at http://www.newton.dep. anl.gov/askasci/gen99/gen99151.htm.

20   *"messing the clock"* LT, 29 May 1916, 10.

20   *"the largest meeting"* LT, 26 February 1918, 3.

20   *"His men had to"* LT, 22 May 1916, 9.

21   *"They play golf"* Edward King, HH 1919, 42.

21   *"approved by the Massachusetts"* This and all citations to the Boston Chamber of Commerce report appear in Boston Chamber of Commerce, "An Hour of Light for an Hour of Night," report of the Special Committee on Daylight Saving Plan, in *Current Affairs* supplement (19 March 1917).

22   *"There are many crops"* NYT, 17 June 1919, letter, 14.

22   *"The Daylight Robbing"* The Nation 109, no. 2825 (23 September 1919): 248.

22   *"was unconstitutional"* NYT, 14 October 1926, 27.

22   *"The equinoctial"* The Nation 108, no. 2806 (12 April 1919): 537.

23   *"the drawback"* LT, 26 February 1918, 3.

24   *"get up at 3:30"* King, HH 1919, 39.

24   *"They cannot ignore"* NYT, 30 April 1925, 20.

24   *"an ungodly hour"* King, HH 1919, 39.

25   *America's human farm population*   This and all other agricultural and demographic data are based on U.S. Census Bureau, *Century and Data Book 2000,* and U.S. Department of Agriculture, "History of American Agriculture 1776–1990," available at usda.gov/history2.

26   *"Upon our American"* North American Review 213 (May 1921): 577.

26   *"meaning the toilers"* NYT, 30 May 1919, 8.

26 *"I would be glad"* James G. Strong, HH 1919, 91.

27 *"The man who wants to"* Ibid., 93.

28 *"I am asking"* King, HH 1919, 35.

28 *"The laboring men"* Roscoe C. McCulloch, HH 1919, 57–58.

29 *"New York is practically"* Marcus Marks, HH 1919, 76.

29 *"solidly against"* Jared Y. Sanders, HH 1919, 79.

29 *"I wonder why"* Marks, HH 1919, 79.

29 *"He spoke of the organization"* Strong, HH 1919, 93.

30 *"in the stately chamber"* NYT, 20 June 1919, 12.

30 *"the International Daylight"* Sydney M. Colgate, HH 1919, 121.

31 *Questioner: It does save* Sydney M. Colgate and various members of Congress, HH 1919, 123–124.

32 *"astonishing change"* NYT, 12 June 1919, 12.

33 *"with the utmost"* James D. Richardson, ed., *A Compilation of the Messages and Papers of the Presidents* (New York: Bureau of Literature, Inc., 1917), 17: 8760–8761, available at "Primary Sources in U.S. History," at www.LexisNexis.com.

33 *"Another Wise One"* NYT, 20 June 1919, 12.

33 *"the supineness"* NYT, 22 August 1919, 10.

Chapter Three: Moon over Miami

35 *"endured it while"* James G. Strong, HH 1919, 94.

35 *"As a matter of fact"* NYT, 31 September 1919, letter, 33.

36 *"We can look forward"* NYT, 2 June 1919, letter, 33.

36 *"God's time is true"* NYT, 29 February 1920, letter, XX7.

36 *"entered the church"* Ibid.

37 *"distinct from natural"* The New Republic, 24 April 1989, 43.

Chapter Four: Banking on the Big Apple

39 *"Contracts great"* NYT, 30 May 1919, 6.

39 *"You cannot have"* Marcus Marks, HH 1919, 76.

40 *Senator William Calder* NYT, 28 September 1919, E2.

40 *"that the confusion"* NYT, 30 May 1919, 6.

40 *"In the minds"* NYT, 23 September 1919, 14.

40 *By 1920, its population* Statistics adapted from Mason Gaffney, "The Resurgence of New York City After 1920," working paper

(Riverside, Calif.: University of California, Riverside, 2001), available at www.economics.ucr.edu/papers.

41   *"New York [was] merely"*   Adapted from accounts of the derivation of the city's nickname, at www.straightdope.com/classics; www.nyhistory.org; and the Museum of the City of New York Web site, at www.mcny.org.

41   *"Congress slipped"*   *NYT,* 24 September 1919, 8.

42   *"it would be impracticable"*   *NYT,* 27 December 1919, 8.

42   *Labor leaders, banks*   *NYT,* 29 September 1919, 4.

42   *"double menace"*   *NYT,* 6 January 1918, 37.

43   *"The greatest industrial"*   *WP,* 23 November 1919, D2.

43   *"Curtailment of passenger"*   *WP,* 8 December 1919, 1.

43   *"The excessive temperature"*   *WP,* 23 November 1919, D2.

44   *"relief of eyestrain"*   *NYT,* 3 February 1921, 19.

44   *"illuminating industry"*   *NYT,* 4 August 1916, 18.

44   *"a serious effect"*   *NYT,* 25 December 1917, 19.

44   *"received information"*   *NYT,* 27 February 1919, 17.

44   *"secret exaggerators"*   *NYT,* 18 July 1919, 10.

44   *"The whole thing"*   "God Knows More About Time Than President Wilson: Letters Against DST," *Scientific American,* 18 October 1919, available at www.historymatters.gmu.edu.

45   *"for here, as nowhere"*   *NYT,* 23 September 1919, 14.

45   *"gasoline interests"*   *NYT,* 18 May 1920, 6.

45   *Nightie Night*   *NYT,* 25 April 1919, 13.

45   *"taking the stand"*   *NYT,* 21 June 1922, 24.

46   *In 1922, the movie*   Adapted from "Growth of Audiences," at www.web.bryant.edu/~history/h364proj; Maggie Valentine, "From Movie Palace to Multiplex," at www.nbm.org/blueprints/90s; and "Film Industry 20's," at www.teaching.arts.usyd.edu.au/history.

46   *"the movie industry"*   V. O. Key, Jr., "American Government and Politics," *American Political Science Review* 30, no. 4 (August 1936): 713–723.

46   *"the history of daylight"*   *The New Republic,* 24 April 1989, 43.

47   *that it "would lead to*   *NYT,* 6 May 1917, 26.

47   *Money makes men bold*   The data on cities and their adoption of Daylight Saving derive from periodic reporting from 1919 to 1930 in *WP* and *NYT.*

47   *The* New York Times *tracked*   *NYT,* 26 March 1920, 17.

48 *"business under this"* NYT, 31 March 1920, 22.

48 *"When am I going"* NYT, 14 April 1921, 3.

49 *"New York State faces"* NYT, 18 May 1920, 6.

49 *Enter Royal S. Copeland* Royal S. Copeland, "Address by Royal S. Copeland, Commissioner of Health, New York City," before State Assembly at Albany, 2 February 1921, reprinted at www.clpgh.org/exhibit/dst.

51 *"in most of the large cities"* WP, 25 April 1921, 1.

51 *"The lesson"* "Progress of the World," *North American Review* 213 (June 1921): 849.

51 *"standard New York City"* NYT, 15 April 1921, 27.

51 *"an unenviable position"* NYT, 25 March 1920, 17.

52 *"discussed measures"* NYT, 27 April 1921, 22.

52 *"that the public display"* NYT, 4 April 1923, 2.

53 *"to set on foot"* NYT, 23 November 1923, 2.

53 *The court ruled against* NYT, 14 October 1926, 27.

53 *"The usual chaos"* "The Time of the World," *North American Review* 222 (July 1928): 108.

54 *"members of the Minneapolis"* WP, 28 April 1929, M2.

55 *"efforts to induce hens"* WP, 18 March 1927, 6.

Chapter Five: Capitol Sports

57 *"swivel-chair"* James G. Strong, HH 1919, 93.

58 *"If the government"* WP, 19 May 1918, SP2.

59 *"By taking advantage"* NYT, 7 April 1918, 29.

59 *"meatless days"* Lillian Rogers Parks, *My Thirty Years Backstairs at the White House* (New York: Fleet Publishing, 1961), quoted by White House Historical Association, "Facts and Trivia" Web page, at http://whitehousehistory.org/06/subs/06_c.html.

60 *Woodrow Wilson . . . fanatic golfer* Based on facts in John Wukovits, "The Golfers in Chief," at www.golfonline.com.

60 *"Bobby Jones"* Alistair Cooke, "Giuliani Receives Knighthood," in *Letter from America*, 12 March 2002, available at www.news.bbc.co.uk.

60 *"Before the daylight"* NYT, 3 September 1919, letter, 12.

61 *"the stroke by stroke"* NYT, 9 September 1919, letter, 16.

61 *"typical corn and hog"* NYT, 26 June 1921, 72.

61 *an industrial statistician* WP, 17 November 1918, 19.

61 *"In order to let"* Strong, HH 1919, 95.

62 *"wearing a Palm Beach"* NYT, 3 July 1921, 1.

62 *"President Harding takes"* Woman Citizen, 20 May 1922, 7.

62 *Congressional Country Club* WP, 26 February 1922, 6.

64 *By 1920, baseball* Adapted from "Baseball Almanac: Year in Review," at www.baseball-almanac.com/yearly.

64 *"the number of night games"* Clifford Blau, "The History of Major League Tie Games," 1997, at www.mysite.verizon.net/brak2.o.

65 *Warren G. Harding was frequently* Based on Wukovits, "The Golfers in Chief," and "Presidential Facts Page," at www.scican.net/~dkochan.

66 *"What this old city"* Woman Citizen, 10 May 1922, 7.

66 *"Irrespective of"* WP, 7 May 1922, 26.

66 *For the next few weeks* The following two paragraphs are based on reporting in WP from April through August 1922.

68 *"golf has lost"* WP, 15 March 1930, 13.

68 *"We suffer most"* H. L. Mencken, *A Carnival of Buncombe: Writings on Politics,* ed. Malcolm Moos (Baltimore: Johns Hopkins, 1956), 136.

68 *Herbert Hoover eschewed* Based on "Herbert Hoover: Hoover-Ball," at www.hoover.archives.gov/education.

68 *"This is a poor taste"* WP, 15 March 1930, 13.

69 *"unmercifully het up"* NYT, 13 June 1929, letter, 14.

69 *When the Depression hit* Based on data from U.S. Census Bureau, *Century and Data Book 2000,* and the National Golf Foundation Web site, www.ngf.org.

CHAPTER SIX: MEAN TIME

71 *When you think* Three Web sites were especially useful sources of calendrical and solar data for this chapter: www.aa.usno.navy.mil/faq; www.webexhibits.org/calendars; and C. J. Hilder, "A Brief History of Time," 1999, at www.teapot.orcon.net.nz.

73 *"If Congress turned"* The Nation 106, no. 2751 (21 March 1918): 308–309.

73 *"In other clocks imported"* NYT, 15 July 1909, 6.

75   *"It sounds boastful"*   WP, 26 April 1985, F4.

76   *"The National Bureau"*   Ibid.

77   *"I address you"*   North American Review 224 (June 1927): 335.

77   *No president and no Congress*   The subsequent account of the development of Standard Time is based on data and historical analysis from the following sources: "A Common Time and First Meridian," *LT,* 4 November 1881, 3; "The Decision of the Prime Meridian Conference," *LT,* 15 October 1884, 9; Sandford Fleming, "The New Method of Measuring Time," *LT,* 4 December 1884, 13; Sandford Fleming, letter to *LT,* 9 January 1897, 12; Sandford Fleming, "Time-Reckoning for the Twentieth Century," in *Smithsonian Report for 1886* (Washington: Byron B. Adams, 1889); "What One Man Did for Time," *WP,* 9 February 1908, M2; "Standard Time," *WP,* 20 June 1937, B6; George Grafton Wilson, "Time and International Law," in *American Journal of International Law* 34, no. 3 (July 1940): 496–497; Ian R. Bartky and Elizabeth Harrison, "Standard and Daylight-Saving Time," *Scientific American* 240, no. 5 (May 1979): 46–52; L. Erik Calonius, "Time Seems to Pass Greenwich By," *Wall Street Journal,* 11 June 1984, 1; Michael Getler, "One Hundred Years of Helpfully Mean Time," *WP,* 27 June 1984, A17; and Clark Blaise, *Time Lord: Sir Sandford Fleming and the Creation of Standard Time* (New York: Pantheon, 2000).

79   *"It was a bold stroke"*   Indianapolis Sentinel, 21 November 1883, quoted in Carlton J. Corliss, *The Day of Two Noons* (Santa Fe: Association of American Railroads, 1952).

80   *"It is a preconceived idea"*   Sandford Fleming, "Time-Reckoning for the Twentieth Century," supplementary note in *Smithsonian Report for 1886* (Washington: Byron B. Adams, 1889).

85   *"The halving of the day"*   Ibid.

86   *"Sunday has been discovered"*   Ibid.

CHAPTER SEVEN: SPLIT DECISIONS

87   *"Opponents did not bother"*   NYT, 15 May 1932, E5.

88   *Georgia refused*   NYT, 29 July 1941, 17.

88   *"cuts theatre receipts"*   "'Unlimited Possibilities for Evil': Hollywood Resists Daylight Saving Time," at www.historymatters.gmu.edu, accessed October 2003.

89 *Californians voted down* NYT, 7 November 1940, 16.

89 *In its initial go at this* WP, 19 November 1918, 6; NYT, 19 November 1918, 15.

90 *Cincinnati felt a little* WP, 21 January 1927, 6.

90 *1932, Chicago traders* NYT, 26 April 1932, 36.

90 *Mrs. Anna Larson* NYT, 25 April 1932, 4.

90 *William Stultz* NYT, 26 April 1932, 42.

91 *New York State Supreme* NYT, 25 September 1929, 2.

91 *Bars and nightclubs* NYT, 19 July 1934, 1.

91 *In Rochester* NYT, 11 May 1937, 27.

91 *By February 1936* WP, 29 February 1936, 2.

92 *And then April* NYT, 27 April 1936, 42.

92 *In August, the ICC* WP, 22 August 1936, X6.

93 *"Yet, in all fairness"* WP, 23 May 1937, B2.

93 *"Its plaintive wail"* WP, 5 May 1937, 1.

93 *"when a man traveled"* WP, 5 September 1937, A6.

93 *"The ether is"* NYT, 26 August 1928, 113.

94 *Live programming* NYT, 14 June 1925, XX16.

95 *Warren G. Harding installed* "Presidential Facts Page," at www.scican.net/~dkochan.

95 *first radio debate* WP, 24 May 1922, 5.

97 Warm Springs Mirror NYT, 1 February 1940, 29.

98 *"Eleven states"* NYT, 25 September 1941, 18.

98 *In 1939, the first* LT, 4 December 1939, 12.

98 *A survey conducted* NYT, 21 May 1941, 25.

99 *in 1942, the entire nation* NYT, 27 December 1941, 14.

99 *In the meantime* The account of the shifting time-zone boundaries in Georgia and Tennessee is based largely on *NYT* reporting: 22 March 1941, 17; 23 March 1941, 36; 23 July 1941, C18; and 21 October 1941, 14.

99 *By then, the ICC* The tally of petitions for time-zone changes is based on figures in Ian R. Bartky and Elizabeth Harrison, "Standard and Daylight-Saving Time," *Scientific American* 240, no. 5 (May 1979): 49.

CHAPTER EIGHT: MEN OF THE HOUR

101 *"now that we are at war* NYT, 28 February 1941, 9.

101 *That summer* "Finance and Economics: Ickes on Power, Gas

Shortage," 28 May 1941, in Facts on File World News Digest Web page, at www.facts.com.

102   *The Office of Production*   NYT, 5 June 1941, 10.

102   *"the first and most"*   LT, 3 February 1942, 3.

102   *Garland was "regarded*   NYT, 16 July 1941, 10.

103   *"I think daylight"*   Ibid.

103   *"need for the establishment"*   Ibid.

103   *"appeals for sacrifices"*   Jonathan Daniels, "A Native at Large," *The Nation*, 6 September 1941, 203.

104   *Although polling since 1937*   NYT, 4 January 1942, 41.

104   *"The Japanese struck"*   WP, 8 February 1942, B3.

105   *"Stephen T. Early"*   NYT, 3 February 1942, 1.

105   *"It is one of the paradoxes"*   This and all other citations to Churchill's essay are from Winston Churchill, "A Silent Toast to William Willett," *Pictorial Weekly*, 28 April 1934, available at www.winstonchurchill.org.

106   *"where the sun's time"*   NYT, 3 April 1921, 3.

106   *For their efforts*   NYT, 24 February 1923, 10.

106   *"the French Cabinet"*   NYT, 1 April 1923, 1.

106   *Every year, a few*   Based on periodic reporting in *LT* and *NYT*.

107   *"witticisms were"*   LT, 6 March 1909, 12.

107   *"pleaded almost"*   Ibid.

107   *"prophesied that a grateful"*   Ibid.

107   *Petts Wood*   LT, 23 May 1927, 11.

108   *"the Father of Daylight"*   NYT, 28 September 1919, E2.

108   *"the acknowledged leader"*   NYT, 28 August 1934, 20.

108   *"I would positively weep"*   Marcus Marks, HH 1919, 76.

109   *"While the daylight-saving"*   Equal Rights, 1 June 1937.

109   *"Marks explained"*   NYT, 9 March 1928, 26.

109   *"regarded as father"*   NYT, 16 July 1941, 10.

110   *"the first commercial body"*   Robert Garland, "Ten Years of Daylight Saving from the Pittsburgh Perspective" (Pittsburgh: Carnegie Library, 1927), 3, available at www.clpgh.org/exhibits/dst.html.

110   *"Paternity of Daylight"*   NYT, 25 July 1941, letter, C14.

110   *"Daylight Saving Act"*   The *LT* index shows that eighteen articles used the phrase in 1908.

110   *Roosevelt settled*   NYT, 21 January 1942, 19.

111   "Months of due succession"   E. J. Edsall, "From the Archives,"

Agape (Calvary Episcopal Church, Pittsburgh), 6 June 2000.

111   *"Only Man is"* NYT, 20 April 1949, 27.

112   *"reported that daylight"* NYT, 16 July 1941, 10.

112   *"Daylight saving time, double"* WP, 8 February 1942, B3.

113   *"Denmark had adopted"* NYT, 30 April 1940, 7, and 16 August 1940, 4.

113   *"Hitler time"* WP, 8 February 1942, B3.

113   *Britain advanced its"* NYT, 5 March 1941, 8.

113   *blackout conditions"* LT, 17 March 1940, 111.

114   *"When it is noon"* WP, 28 February 1942, B3.

114   *"for the purpose of"* NYT, 30 June 1917, 1.

114   *he outlawed the seven-day*   Based on LT reporting and data from www.webexhibits.org/calendars.

115   *"Change Your Clocks"*   Thomas Kent, "Spring Forward—Warily," Associated Press report, 29 March 1981.

115   *"confirmed that the introduction"*   "The Soviet Union Goes on Daylight Savings [sic] Time," United Press International report, 1 April 1981.

115   *"Estonia, Latvia, and"*   "Solar Time to Be Used," TASS report, 20 October 1988.

115   *"Soviet officials admit"*   Wall Street Journal, 22 March 1991, A6.

116   *"red-faced Soviet"*   Toronto Star, 22 March 1991, A2.

116   *"Are We Going to"*   Ibid.

116   *"forgot to return"*   National Review, 43, no. 16 (9 September 1991): 35.

116   *"To call Moscow's"* NYT, 13 October 1991, letter, 14.

117   *"Administrations of 40"*   "Russia to Revert," TASS report, 13 January 1992.

118   *"The cattle lose"*   Moscow Times, 30 October 1999, 1.

CHAPTER NINE: OUT OF UNIFORM

120   *the Michigan legislature* NYT, 14 February 1923, R7.

120   *War Production Board* NYT, 23 February 1945, 12.

120   *Cole of Missouri* NYT, 27 June 1943, 23.

121   *5 billion kilowatt* NYT, 15 July 1945, 44.

121   *"Even before the Congress"* NYT, 18 August 1945, 13.

121   *The 1945 Gallup poll* WP, 14 September 1945, 11.

121 *In 1946, the state of Virginia* WP, 19 March 1946, 7.

122 *These maneuvers* WP, 19 May 1946, B3.

122 *"The long-distance"* Ibid.

123 *Although by 1950* State and national trends derive from reports in NYT (10 March 1948, 29; 12 December 1948, E7; 6 March 1949, 40; 8 April 1949, 270); WP (29 September 1947, 4; 24 April 1948, 2; 11 January 1949, 10); and "The Rains Came," *The Nation,* 27 March 1948, 347.

123 *"Mount San Jacinto"* NYT, 8 November 1946, 25.

124 *"leaving Maryland"* WP, 12 September 1949, B12.

124 *"The railways at their"* LT, 1 May 1950, 6.

125 *The Japanese were* Monumenta Nipponica 50, no. 1 (April 1991): 103–116; NYT, 11 April 1991, A24.

125 *Chungking* NYT, 26 April 1945, 16.

126 *General John Hodge* NYT, 25 May 1948, 15.

126 *"a symbol by which"* NYT, 23 April 1955, 18.

126 *"the thousands of dollars"* NYT, 23 February 1956, 19.

126 *However, the beleaguered* NYT, 29 March 1957, 14.

127 *Harley O. Staggers* WP, 17 February 1956, 2.

127 *Wisconsin* NYT, 4 April 1957, 21.

127 *Minnesota* NYT, 24 April 1957, 35.

127 *Kentucky* NYT, 4 March 1960, 1.

127 *"In the course of"* NYT, 12 July 1959, 74.

128 *"The Interstate Commerce"* NYT, 8 January 1960, 17.

128 *"Times have changed"* Ibid.

CHAPTER 10: LAWMAKERS AND JAWBREAKERS

129 *By the early 1960s* The principal sources for this chapter are the U.S. House and Senate hearings in the abbreviations list. Most important was HH 1966, which includes three passages from which I have drawn many facts and anecdotes: a written statement from Robert Ramspeck, national chairman of the Committee for Time Uniformity, 61–73; the testimony of Robert E. Redding, executive director of the Committee for Time Uniformity, 73–78; and the full text of Thomas Pyne, "A Worldwide Survey of Time Observance," prepared for the Committee on Time Uniformity, 78–84.

131 *"We have, I am sure"* Thomas N. Frost, HH 1966, 77.

131 *"one of the major"* Sam Bresnahan, "Time After Time," (*University of Virginia*) *Cavalier Daily*, 2 April 2001.

132 *"that for three days"* *Wall Street Journal*, 23 October 1992, A12.

133 *"received suggestions"* William G. Colman, SH 1963, 7.

134 *"The widespread time"* *NYT*, 30 April 1963, 54.

135 *"I would not propose"* Robert E. Redding, HH 1966, 59.

135 *"It is, of course"* Joseph E. Karth, HH 1966, 25.

137 *"because many people trying"* Kenneth J. Gray, HH 1966, 47.

137 *"the confusion encountered"* *NYT*, 31 March 1996, A5.

137 *"the first peacetime"* Ibid.

138 *a few skirmishes* WP, 9 September 1967, A5.

138 *"A child gets up"* *NYT*, 27 February 1967, 14.

138 *state of Indiana* HH 1966; and Monroe County (Indiana) Community School Corporation, *What Time Is It in Indiana?* curriculum project, Monroe County (Indiana) Community School Corporation, available at www.mccsc.edu.

139 *"First, . . . it would authorize"* This and all other citations to Nixon's televised speech are from Richard Nixon, "Address to the Nation About Policies to Deal with the Energy Shortages," 7 November 1973, in *Public Papers of the Presidents of the United States, 1973* (Washington: Government Printing Office, 1975).

140 *By 1970, most Americans* Several characterizations of the energy crisis were adapted from "Energy Policy, 1973–1976, Legislative Overview (1977)," in *Congress and the Nation, 73–76*, vol. 4 (Washington: CQ Press [CQ Electronic Library, CQ Public Affairs Collection], 1977).

141 *"Most people don't"* *NYT*, 7 January 1974, 65.

141 *Within a week* *NYT*, 14 January 1974, 21.

141 *The Edison Electric* *NYT*, 17 January 1974, 81.

141 *"We use up"* *NYT*, 18 January 1974, 33.

142 *"six of the deaths"* *NYT*, 31 January 1974, 13.

142 *school bus in Atlanta* *NYT*, 2 February 1974, 16.

142 *"that in the first three"* *Oakland (Calif.) Post*, 13 February 1974, 1.

142 *Idaho and Oregon* *NYT*, 6 January 1974, 52.

142 *"to lead our country"* Tim Lee Carter, HH 1974, 5.

142 *"You can legislate"* Robert Price, HH 1974, 14.

143 *The Department of Transportation's report* Ian Bartky, "Analysis of DOT Study (July 1974)," HH 1974, 32–44.

143 *"The definition of daylight"* Charles G. Rose, HH 1974, 25.

145 *"It could save"* Silvio O. Conte, HH 1985, 12.

146 *"a net decline. . . . This limited"* Richard F. Walsh, HH 1985, 26.

146 *"impossible to conclude"* Ibid., 26.

146 *"found that a two-month"* Ibid., 19–20.

147 *"actual clock times"* Ibid., 22.

148 *"the barbecue lifestyle"* Arthur Seeds, HH 1985, 69. The testimony of Seeds follows testimony from several other members of the Daylight Saving Time Coalition trade association; the details used in this chapter appear in HH 1985, 45–53 and 55–91.

149 *"opportunity to impact"* Fran Denman Counihan, HH 1985, 53.

149 *"Mindy has to get home"* Ibid., 63.

150 *"At home"* Wendell H. Ford, SH 1985, 22.

150 *"If [consumers] buy more"* Ibid., 52.

150 *"Today is Halloween"* Slade Gorton, SH 1985, 53.

151 *"Go out during daylight"* Peter Pantuso, SH 1985, 54.

151 *pumpkin filled with candy* "Hear All About It!" Lifestyles section, PR Newswire, 26 October 1999.

Chapter Eleven: Millennial Fever

153 *In November 1998* Details of the shifting date line are based on comparisons of maps, atlases, and encyclopedia entries and the four sources that follow immediately.

153 *Tonga adopted* "The Time That Land Forgot," *Sydney Morning Herald,* 20 November 2002.

153 *The British Royal Geographic* "Who's on First," *World Press Review* 46, no. 1 (January 1998): 38.

154 *"the change was made"* "Dawn of a New Era Pits Pacific Islands in Race Against Time," *Wall Street Journal,* 22 January 1996, A1.

154 *"The first point"* "Dawn of an Era," *Canadian Geographic Annual* 120, no. 1 (2000): 25.

155 *Iran* NYT, 11 July 1977, 47; Siamak Movahedi, "Cultural Perceptions of Time," *Comparative Studies in Society and History* 27, no. 3 (1979): 385–400.

155 *Israel . . . air raids* NYT, 22 May 1948, 2.

155 *Morning rituals* LT, 22 April 1981, 6.

156 *Energy experts* NYT, 7 April 1986, A7.

156 *"They demonstrated"*   *The Guardian,* 7 April 1986.

156 *127 days*   Based on reporting in the *Jerusalem Post* and *Financial Times.*

156 *"another dividing line"*   *Jerusalem Report,* 17 April 1997, 10.

156 *"In Palestinian areas"*   *Financial Times,* 4 September 1999, 3.

157 *In 1986, having collapsed*   *Toronto Star,* 5 May 1986.

157 *Standard Time in 1992*   *San Francisco Chronicle,* 2 April 1999, A8.

158 *"allowing employees"*   *Mainichi Shimbun,* 7 July 2003, 2.

159 *"more sunshine"*   "In France, Two Hours Ahead of the Sun," United Press International report, 26 March 2002.

159 *"who are still in"*   "Many European Countries Go on Summer Time This Weekend," Associated Press report, 29 March 1985.

159 *"it is less and less"*   *U.S. News & World Report,* 16 September 1996, 18.

160 *In 1946*   *LT,* 13 April 1946, 4.

160 *Scotland*   *The Scotsman,* 12 November 1994, letter, 12.

160 *Utsjoki*   "East of (Sw)eden," at www.dlc.fi/wmoore/fin.

161 *Policy Studies*   Mayer Hillman, *Time for Change: Setting Clocks Forward by One Hour Throughout the Year* (London: Policy Studies Institute, 1993).

162 *"We don't want it"*   *Northern Miner,* 28 February 2003, 3.

163 *"Doesn't poor old"*   *Maclean's,* 9 May 1988, letter, 6.

163 *"had long lobbied"*   *NYT,* 14 August 1989, A4.

163 *"because their northern"*   "International News," Associated Press report, 3 April 1998.

163 *Free Trade Agreement*   "A Change of Tiempo in Mexico," *Economist* 8 (March 2001); *NYT,* 3 April 1999.

164 *"no one was prepared"*   *Washington Times,* 23 October 1997, A21.

164 *"U.S. demands"*   *Ottawa Citizen,* 14 October 1997, A12.

164 *Brazil annually*   Based on reporting from Global News Wire, Business News Americas, and *Financial Times.*

165 *Argentina*   *Argentina Weekly,* 28 May 2004, 1; "Power in Latin America," *Financial Times Energy Newsletter,* 5 July 2000, 14.

165 *"Sunday, October 29"*   Proclamation 6057, *Federal Register,* 54 FR 46041 (Washington: Government Printing Office, 1989).

165 *"I have three types"*   *NYT,* 5 April 1995, letter, A24.

166 *"public education campaign"*   *Ad Week,* 12 March 1990, 29.

166 *Amtrak*   *NYT,* 17 November 1984, 23.

167 *"How come they never"* St. Petersburg Times, 1 April 1988, 1B.

167 *Representative Brad Sherman* Las Vegas Review-Journal, 26 May 2001; House of Representatives Committee on Science, press release, 24 May 2001.

168 *"If it becomes law"* Houston Chronicle, 24 May 2001, 1.

168 *"They can do it"* Ibid.

168 *"Imagine the growling"* Jewish Exponent, 209, no. 23 (7 June 2001): 12.

169 *Woolsey: How are we* Lynn C. Woolsey, HH 2001, 27.

170 *"In 1984, I founded"* James C. Benfield, HH 2001, 20–21.

170 *"In summary"* Ibid., 22.

170 *"I am more confused"* Woolsey, HH 2001, 26.

Index